Anne Carson
Wrong Norma

Also by Anne Carson
Available from New Directions

The Albertine Workout

Antigonick

Bakkhai

Glass, Irony and God

H of H Playbook

Norma Jeane Baker of Troy

Nox

The Trojan Women (with Rosanna Bruno)

Wrong Norma

Anne Carson

wrong norma

a new directions book

Some of the pieces in this book previously appeared in Andrea Büttner, *Beggars* (Koenig Books, London, 2019); *Granta*; *Harper's Magazine*; *London Review of Books*; *The New Yorker*; *The New York Review of Books*; *The Paris Review*; and *Tin House*.

First published as New Directions Paperbook 1583 in 2024

Manufactured in China

Design by Anne Carson and Laura Lindgren

Library of Congress Cataloging-in-Publication Data
Names: Carson, Anne, 1950– author.
Title: Wrong Norma / Anne Carson.
Description: First edition. | New York : New Directions Books, 2024.
Identifiers: LCCN 2023030048 | ISBN 9780811230346 (paperback) |
    ISBN 9780811230353 (ebook)
Subjects: LCGFT: Poetry.
Classification: LCC PS3553.A7667 W76 2024 | DDC 811/.54—dc23/
    eng/20230720
LC record available at https://lccn.loc.gov/2023030048

10 9 8 7 6 5 4 3 2 1

New Directions Books are published for James Laughlin
by New Directions Publishing Corporation
80 Eighth Avenue, New York 10011

CONTENTS

have
the
blackbird
eye the sandwich

have
everyone them
busy
on deck

have

think
they see land

have
vastness
be
of sea be simply missing

1 = 1

Before the others are up, dawn, she walks to the lake, listening to Bach, the first clavichord exercise, which she plans to have played at her funeral someday, has had this plan since she first heard the music, and thinking of it she weeps lightly. The lake is whipped by wind and tides (big lake) doing what tides do, she never knows in or out. There is a man standing onshore and a big dog swimming back to him, stick in mouth. This repeats. The dog does not tire. She peels a swim cap onto her head, goggles, enters the water, which is cold but not shocking. Swims. High waves in one direction. The dog is gone. Now she is alone. There is a mental pressure to swim well and to use this water correctly. People think swimming is carefree. Just a bath! In fact it is full of anxieties. Every water has its own rules and offering. Misuse is hard to explain. Perhaps involved is that commonplace struggle to know beauty, to know beauty exactly, to put oneself right in its path, to be in the perfect place to hear the nightingale sing, see the groom kiss the bride, clock the comet. Every water has a right place to be but this place is in motion, you have to keep finding it, keep having it find you. Your movement sinks into and out of it with each stroke. You can fail it with each stroke. What does that mean, fail it?

After a while she climbs out over stones, puts on small flippers, reenters the water. The difference is like the difference between glimpsing a beautiful thing and staring at it. Now she can stream into the way of the water and stay there. She stays. She is one of the most selfish people she has ever known, she thinks about this while swimming and after, on the beach, in her towel, shivering. It is an aspect of personality hard to change. Generous gestures, when she attempts them, seem to swipe through the lives of others like a random bear paw, often making matters worse. And she finds no momentum in sharing, in benevolence, in charity, no interaction with another person ever brought her a bolt of pure aliveness like entering the water on a still morning with the world empty in every direction to the sky. That first entry. Crossing the border of consciousness into, into what?

And then the (she searches for it) *instruction* of balancing along in the water, the ten thousand adjustments of vivid action, the staining together of mind and time so that she is no longer miles and miles apart from her life watching it differently unfold but *in* it, *as* it, *it*. Not at all like meditation - a common analogy - but almost forensic. An application of attention, at the same time autonomic, these modes being not exclusive of one another. Swimming has a stoniness, water being as different from air as stones. You find your way among its structures, its ancientness, its history as an entity without response to you and yet complicit in the intrusion. You have no personhood there and water is uninterested in itself, stones don't care if you tell their story nicely - or yours. The irrational bowels, luck at cards, love of your mother, well-crafted similes, all are lost in the slide from depth to depth, pure, impure, compassionless. There is no renunciation in this (cf. meditation), no striving to detach, all these things, all the things you can name, being simply gone. Meaning, gone.

Her lake visit ends. Back at home, the newspapers, front-page photos of a train car in Europe jammed floor to door with escaped victims of a war zone further south, people denied transit. Filthy families and souls in despair pressed flat against one another in the grip to survive, uncountable arms and legs, torn-open eyes, locked all night in a train waiting for dawn, a scene so much the antithesis of her own morning she cannot think it. What sense it makes for these two mornings to exist side by side in the world where we live - should this be framed as a question - would not be answerable by philosophy or poetry or finance or the shallows or the deeps of her own mind, she fears. Words like *rationale* become, well, laughable. Rationales have to do with composite things - migrants, swimmers, the selfish, the damned, the plural - but existence and sense belong to singularity. Sentences are strategic. They let you off.

She goes downstairs and out to the stoop, hoping it's cooler there. Traffic crashes past. Chandler is on the sidewalk making a chalk drawing. *Comrade Chandler*, she says. He doesn't look up. *What's the drawing?* He goes on chalking. His gaze is ahead and within. He lives in back of the house somewhere, speaks not much, draws a lot. She calls him Comrade because she'd been reading Russian books the summer she met him and she thought him secretive. This was an error. Secrecy implies a concern for one's own personality. You hardly ever saw Chandler enter a room, he's just there, or leave a room, he seeps away, small tide of person, noticed as a retraction.

She stands nearer. The drawing is a pear tree. She can see the pears all over it, small perfect green chalk globes with yellow-cream-white highlights. She wants to lean down and bite them. *You've hit the nail on the head here, Comrade*, she says. He doesn't answer. Once they had a conversation, extending over many months, in broken bits, about mushrooms. He'd said the thing he hated about being in jail was the mushrooms. For several days she wondered if he meant the food, but it didn't make sense they served mushrooms in jail often enough to be a problem, or if he had a damp cell with fungus sprouting in the corners, but this too seemed extreme, and gradually she understood him to mean he had been able to see a patch of mushrooms, boletes, from one of the jail windows and he used to go hunting for those in the woods with his mother when he was a kid and it made him sad. Not a mushroom fancier herself she didn't have anything subjective to say at the time so she told him John Cage was a mushroom hunter too, with his mom, when a kid, and wrote a book about it, a sort of mushroom guide, that she could lend him. Chandler had not answered. She wasn't sure he read books or knew who John Cage was. Conversation is precarious. Now, looking at the very round chalky pale pears, mushrooms come to mind again and she says, *One day John Cage was out mushrooming with his mother and after an hour or so she turns to him and says, We can always go to the store and buy some real ones.*

Silence from Chandler. He is adding touches of red to the pear array, here or there. Then suddenly all his five teeth laugh. The laugh slams out of him and is gone. He returns to chalking. *Quickenough quickenough*, muttering to himself, and something something *buttended* something. She goes back to the stoop and stands on the bottom step. Evening now. Still hot. *Long day, Chandler*, she says to the back of his head. He's moving down the sidewalk to mark out a new drawing. Red chalk in hand, it will be a fox, he likes a fox at the end of the day.

Upstairs she finds herself thinking again about the failure to swim. It can be quantitative as well as qualitative. Imagine how many pools, ponds, lakes, bays, streams, stretches of swimmable shore there are in the world right now, probably half of them empty of swimmers by reason of night or negligence. Empty, still, perfect. The waste, the extravagance - why not make oneself accountable to that? Why not swim in all of them? One by one or all at once, geographically or conceptually, putting aside gleaming

Burt Lancaster, someone should be using all that water. Across the level ocean of her mind come floating certain refugees in a makeshift plastic boat so crowded with passengers they are stacked in layers and dropping over the sides. She had seen this picture. She had read that larger ships might sail very near, that they would stop to consider the woe and the odds, then keep going. Sometimes bottles of water or biscuits were tossed from the larger ships before they started their engines again. What could she put against the desolation of that moment, watching the ship start its engines again. What is the price of desolation and who pays. Some questions don't warrant a question mark.

Passengers. To pass. To pass muster. To pass over. To be passed over. To pass the buck. To pass the butter. To pass out. To pass to one's reward. She is eating yogurt when the doorbell rings. *Didn't know that bell worked*, she says, wiping her mouth with her sleeve as she gets to the door. Comrade Chandler gestures with his head toward downstairs. They descend. *Got yogurt on your eyebrow*, he says over his shoulder. *Oh*, she says, *thanks*. The finished fox drawing is under a streetlamp. It glows. He has used some sort of phosphorescent chalk and the fox, swimming in a blue-green jellylike lucidity of its own, is escaping all possible explanations. She stares at the blue-green. It has clearness, wetness, coolness, the deep-lit self-immersedness of water. *You made a lake*, she says, turning to him, but he is gone, now that it's night, off to wherever he goes when he is once again absolved. She stands awhile watching the fox swim, looking back on the day, pouring in and out. To be alive is just this pouring in and out. Ethics minimal. Try to swim without thinking how it looks. Beware mockery, mockery is too easy. She feels a breeze on her forehead, a night wind. The fox is stroking splashlessly forward. The fox does not fail.

what is your philosophy of time
backwards is north.
what is your philosophy of time
just smile
what is your philosophy of time
as a noun (snare) as a verb (flick flip twirl)

AN EVENING WITH JOSEPH CONRAD

Once somehow, once somehow I lost both of them, a man was saying as he came out of the elevator that morning. He was alone. He flicked his eyes on me, off me. He had a furtive tinge and a swank black overcoat - I thought at once of Joseph Conrad, as he is in formal photographs, with the not-quite-Western eyes and virtuosic goatee.

Once I was invited to a christening in a country far away. It was June. On the drive the weather closed in, grey and vague, typical summer weather for that region. The ceremony was in a tiny white church. Everyone sat packed like teeth. Short glorious off-key songs were sung by a ten-year-old girl. The sun came out. Everyone rushed from the church to stand amid graves, talking, amazed. Vast general fields reached away on every side to the mountains, a greenness so dazzling it hurt the eyes. Soon all embarked in cars and drove to a nearby farmhouse for lunch. Sunlight was spilling over everything. The farmhouse stood with all doors open, children tumbling in and out, busy conversation everywhere. I knew scarcely anyone, so stood in an inner room, near a table draped in a lace cloth and heavy with cakes. If I were Joseph Conrad, I could not help thinking, I would be mastering this room in case I might one day write about it. There stood a cake as big as two schoolbooks emblazoned with the name of the new baby; a cake in chocolate shaped like a bear full of candies that erupted for children; several tall blocklike structures layered with red jam alongside fluffy cream cakes and other smaller foods, shrimps on crackers and so forth. Finally, carried in late with a sort of hasty deference, on its own blue-patterned china plate, a stack of sliced white bread. The plate was placed, as it happened, in a shaft of sunlight and the white bread shone, as white as a freshly laundered cuff, as white as its own piety, on the lace cloth in that shadowy room. There was something ultimate, adorable, almost sexual, something certainly historical, in that stack of bread set into the larger history of a sunlit afternoon on that ancient property amid fields stretching to the ends of the mind. No one ate the white bread. It wasn't there to be eaten. It was a chapter of civilization. Joseph Conrad, who had lived that chapter, now groping in his pocket for the small notebook in which he liked to record thoughts, would find he'd left it back at the hotel.

Once Conrad shot himself in the chest. Not much is known about that.

Once a student of mine, translating Euripides on a mid-term exam, came up with "wild in the grips of a god." Those were the days.

Once Thomas Hardy was strolling on the heath with a telescope. He put the telescope to his eye. He saw a man in white on the gallows at Dorchester and at that moment the man dropped down and the town clock struck eight. "Faintly," says his autobiography. A faint note from the town clock. A man has lost things.

Once I wondered if white is a colour.

Once you touched Thomas Hardy he recoiled, so a child-hood playmate records. This peculiarity never left him. I doubt he offered to shake hands with Joseph Conrad when introduced to him in the drawing room of Charles Hag-berg Wright on a January night of 1907. It was a dinner for the Gorkys, who were late.

Once I was waiting for the elevator in my building and Joseph Conrad came walking out.

Once I began wondering about history, I couldn't escape the feeling that we only call it history when things go wrong.

Once a reporter wrote of "the miracle of white bread" in a *valuta* store in Moscow - this glowing heap of crisp little loaves twice as radiant as the rubies and diamonds of the jewellery department at the other end of the shop (Eugene Lyons, *Assignment in Utopia*, 1937).

Once I spent a season impersonating Joseph Conrad. Dressed in a large overcoat I would emerge from the elevator, hoping to catch myself waiting for me. He was hot in my coat.

Once Goethe called colour "a degree of darkness."

Once I encountered the term "counterespionage," I became confused about what "espionage" was. How many sides can a piece of paper have? Why put a mirror *behind* your head (Freud did)? When I wish to report that I, as Joseph Conrad, never pick up the check in a restaurant, whose dossier do I put it in?

Once Charles Hagberg Wright realized the Gorkys were going to be not just late but very late, did he try to get a conversational crackle going between Thomas Hardy and Joseph Conrad? History is blank.

Once I was sitting and wondering about the mirror behind Freud's head when a letter dropped through the mail slot, inviting me to a christening in a country far away. Aha! I thought: I would send Joseph Conrad.

Once I relaxed about counterespionage I began to enjoy gazing down through layers of Joseph Conrad going about his faint, preconscious tasks. Several ladies at the christening found his faintness attractive. Standing by the cake table chatting about the blue of the sea, the tumbling of the sea, redemption by sea, he did not let on, nor did I, how gloomy it made him to be the guy to go to for *all this sea stuff*, whereas Thomas Hardy published novel after novel on any topic he liked and they sold and kept selling.

Once the analysis is over, said Freud to H.D., the person is dead. And H.D. said, Which person?

Once Patroklos fell, did the horses of Akhilles see colour for the first time?

Once I was doing badly and read Lacan for help. *Ce que je cherche dans la parole, c'est la réponse de l'autre,* I read. *Ce qui me constitue comme sujet, c'est ma question.* I felt better already. Next came a bit of French I couldn't construe. I flipped to the endnotes and found:

ably 1b view ad w11t w111 ie. 1b

ar1er ta d1b1 11d

Once the party had ended and I was clearing plates with the hostess, I asked her about the white bread, its signifying supremacy, its itinerary as a fetish, I may even have quoted Lacan. She laughed. No, it was just a mistake. Her sister had misheard her on the phone, she'd been exasperated at first but then it didn't matter, there were too many cakes anyway.

what is your philosophy of time
me and D switching beds

CLIVE SONG

If I were an early person
I'd look for the limits of human wisdom
by going to sacred oak trees
or the local blind man with lips on fire.
But this is now. This is NYC.
I go to Clive.
We meet in a diner
and queue for the breakfast special.
Clive's British.
He tries to make the large Hispanic short-order cook appreciate "underdone"
French toast. "My wife told me
not to say *soggy*," says Clive.
We pay. Currie shows up.
We sit and talk
of Clive's next trip to Guantanamo where,
although he's visited 56 times, they're questioning
(this time) his signature.
He laughs.
His current client, a Moroccan man,
has been cleared for release
and also informed
he will never leave.
Clive, a lawyer, questions the logic of this.
"I shouldn't laugh."
He tells more stories.
"Evidence" at Guantanamo comes often from snitches.
When the same snitch brought evidence
against 300 different people,
Clive wondered about motive
and did some research. The fact was,
each time the guy snitched
he got a free pass to "the love shack"

where the Americans show porn.
Clive plans to question   ·
the number 300
on statistical grounds.
Most of us know only 300 people
in the whole world, demographers say.
If you think like a lawyer
you find the limits of human wisdom
in facts like that.
His French toast arrives.
"Is it underdone?" I ask. He sighs
and tells
of his son at home who's obsessed with *The Goon Show*.
I don't think like a lawyer.
I'm looking to see
how the sacred oaks come whispering through a man like Clive,
now striving for people on death row or places like Gitmo
for 35 years,
but worried
his son doesn't see the merits of *Monty Python*
or grasp its direct descent from the Goons.
I imagine a tumbling squabbling family
back home in the Midlands.
Clive looks at his watch.
I take scraps of French toast to the trash.
We'll meet again.
He likes the idea
(Currie's idea)
of travelling around Pakistan with a troop of square dancers.
Because the square dance is a "greeting dance"
and we need more greeting! Clive smiles
and goes up the street
in his saggy-butt pants,
looking not much like a high-powered lawyer,

and the limits of human wisdom remain
(as we who confuse the greetings of dogs and gods
prefer limits
do) more
or less
where they were.

what is your philosophy of time
power
what is your philosophy of time
for a year I made homemade toothpaste

how do you sustain morale during a long project
by loosing track
how do you sustain morale during a long project
put full faith in Ricky

Dear Krito, don't come today. If you do I'll have to pretend to be asleep or ashamed or explain why I sent my wife home. Tears are all about the weeper, aren't they? My kid has more sense. She was here, took one look around, said, *It's really damp in this place you need a hat*, came back a half hour later with that woolly cap you gave me last winter. I like practical people. My death is set for three days hence. There's nothing you can do. But let me thank you for the hemlock. I know it wasn't cheap with the bribes and the tax - why can't they just grow the stuff in this country? - but God, it's better than the other way, the so-called bloodless crucifixion, with the stakes and the iron collar. No one wants to see another person die like that - Krito, you'd have nightmares for years. And I sort of like the idea of just numbing out. I've been numb for years according to my wife - it was the only way to bear her - oh that was unkind. I've been unkind for years, at home anyway, funny how the worst self comes out there. My life is guys, you know that! guys and drinking. I'm a talker. I believe in talk - rip the lids off! let all the cats out of all the bags! - though most of what I say's just common sense. Do I frighten people? Saying there's no back wall? Nothing between you and your heart of darkness? Or if there is, you can't pray to it, you can't write poems about it, you can't compete for its love. It smells of terrible plans and nonexistence. Sorry, dramatic. Speaking of terrible plans, though, don't let Plato come to visit me. He'll start quoting stuff I said in the old days, I shudder to hear it. Or he'll lecture me on The Law. *It's not the law putting you to death, it's the lawyers*, he'll say and I'll say, *Nice distinction but*. Then he'll go on about swans or gymnastics or who knows what, he'll go on, go on, go on - whenever I talk to our dear Plato I feel I'm drifting into eternity, you know what I mean. Or maybe you don't. You're an odd one, Krito. You look like Bob Dylan with your little gold eyes and your skinny arms. And you just love arguments, am I right? When did I stop caring about arguments? Because I did, I stopped. My mind is blank as bread. Maybe it's the hum in here. That humming, do you hear it? is it in the walls or in my ears? Voices, voices, it's there all the time, voices with no words. It drowns out every other sound. Remember the old days when they'd play Iggy Pop all night to break the prisoners down? That was when the war was on; the beast is dozing now. Anyway, if you were here I might not be able to get what you're saying - on the other hand, beloved Krito, if you do come, can you bring another one of those woolly caps? I gave mine to the guard. He looked miserable. It's really damp in this place.

(letter from Sokrates in gaol)

and bit someone. Too bad it was Virginia Woolf. Who rallied the locals who rallied the local magistrate who said destroy the dog. Locals appalled. Oh we don't want it destroyed, just restrained. Poor Maudes, they said. Need their dog. So how'd it turn out? Eddy says. ~~She tells him she doesn't know.~~ *I don't know* VW cuts the anecdote off right there. Eddy makes a *hmmm* sound, goes back to work.

But the dog! the dog! she wants to say. ~~Just let it go.~~ I hate when people bare their souls, early remark of his she'd tucked away.

EDDY

Funny thing to worry about. Little hairs. Hairs on back of sweater as she goes out of the room. Little hairs, how you look from the back, girls worry about this. Or they used to. Now girls are free. Okay to be unpretty, ungirls. She thinks back. Freedom. Her first airplane to Europe. Scholarship girl. This term was used. Heady sense of a lightly exotic self, chatting with older man as plane lifts, accepting a whiskey, feeling his hand on her knee. Cold yeast of that moment. Please remove your hand. Not exactly shame. What is shame. A matter of temperatures. Heat flooding the neck, ears. Cross your legs, don't cross your legs, what is he thinking now, now you must stay awake, the long night a black window. His air vent blowing on her, just put up with it, little hairs riffling on forehead, that was years ago. That was innocence. Not that her sexual aptitudes have enlarged or she learned to like whiskey. No. You've got a funny look, Eddy is saying, what's wrong? Nothing, she says. She'd come in again and sat and swallowed an earring, having found a pair in her pocket and put one in her mouth while poking the other through. Just a small one, sort of a pearl. Nothing, she repeats.

~~~

Does ceiling bloodspatter relate to a homicide or not, he is running tests. Could be just residue of life in the house, he says, it's a drug house. Addicts clear blood from the needle that way. But on the other hand, so do paramedics. Really? Clear the syringe, yes. Odd how you use *needle* for addicts and *syringe* for medics, she says. Eddy looks at her. She goes back to emailing, what he hired her for. Calm as linen is the lab at night, lamps on, black winter beating the windows.

~~~

That was before I knew you is a phrase that steals into people's idiom vaguely. Thus are eras. She and Eddy do not live together. But when not with him she feels a bit wrong. Horizons get loud. Men throwing chair after chair into a bin below her window just before daybreak. Night and its stars soak slowly backwards out of the world as she goes klipklopping along in the dawn, hearing the pure strike of bootheels on snow. Thinking sonnets. Thinking other people's suffering. Who has a right to it. The masters don't ask. Just lift the knife and cut. Virginia Woolf for example - not sonnets but a master cutter. That story about the Maude family. Lived down the street from VW. Their dog, she was telling Eddy the other day, the Maudes got a dog because they couldn't pay their bills. Made no sense to Eddy. She tried to explain to him what "frighten duns" meant and how one day the dog ran out and bit someone. Too bad it was Virginia Woolf. Who rallied the locals, who rallied the local magistrate, who said destroy the dog. Locals appalled. Oh we don't want it destroyed, just restrained. Poor Maudes, they said. Need their dog. So how'd it turn out? Eddy says. I don't know, she says, VW cuts the anecdote off right there. Eddy makes a *hmmm* sound, goes back to work.

But the dog! the dog! she wants to say.

~~~

She'd followed him out the back door of a lecture. Originally. Curious. Parking lot. By the bins. Plastic wad from his pocket. Unwrapped it, took out five little somethings and arranged them one by one on top of the bins. Came from the air above the trees a big swanking blackness and *wham wham wham* five somethings are gone and so is the blackness. His crow.

~~~

It had been an odd lecture. Lot of noise from the dining room next door, an evening event being clattered into place. He was a good lecturer, knew how to tap his voice in under other sounds. Knew blood. She'd come for the slides, didn't care about DNA, forensics, wanted to sit in the dark and not think.

~~~

(he turned from the bins)
you following me
no
go get us a drink then

~~~

And she at a stuck place for a while now, about a year, trying to make a sonnet cycle about a subject she didn't feel able to - raise the knife and cut? Detainment, enhancement, asymmetry, the official words so shrewdly drained of connection to real life. DENK ES GENAU she copied onto the cover of her notebook. Was that the problem? To think it exact? Think exact about the stitching. She could not, she stopped. There were photographs, sites, information. But the pain exactly. What was her question about the pain? Exact question. She started, started, started again, stopped. Who was this boy, light from a decayed star for all she knew dead already, a photograph she'd seen once and couldn't find again. She imagined him, she stopped. What right had she? His day, his lips, his instruments. His aftermath. She made it be winter for him (in one sonnet), it was winter for her. She made this fiction of simultaneity between them then stopped, unholy. Her real minutes, his - who knows? Was it all about her, of course it was. No. Two big bloody stitches one each side of the cupid's bow. Not her.

Yet how effective it might have been - a boy's atrocious bloody boredom, her own virtuoso stanzas of six and eight, all the steaming, stinking heap of it urged into rhyme, she stopped. Ashamed. Starving to do it. She read up on poetry of witness and telling the truth to power and thought, no. Sassoon, Celan, "you told me how you butchered prisoners . . ." all that, no. "Your golden hair . . ." no. Poems don't purify anyone. There is a heap. It steams and stinks. *Denk es genau* she'd read in Ernst Meister, a poet who all his life suffered from not being Paul Celan. No. She stopped. And then felt so righteous she had to go out on a long walk to quiet the churning. Ending up at a lecture.

~~~

what would he use for thread
to stitch it you mean
yes
any old piece of wire from around the cell, I guess, a shoelace

what about the needle
be surprised what addicts will use to get through skin
he wasn't an addict
I'm just saying
just saying what (she watches him count bolts into a bag)
why not have a needle smuggled in, even a big one, easy
I hate the light in here this grey light
really? hardware store's one of my favourite places
I got that
how do you
what
never mind let's go

~~~

It was some time before she knew if Eddy was a first or last name.
She never did finish the sonnets, never did find out more, enough,
about the boy who sewed his lips shut in a refugee camp because he
was out of his mind with pain and rage, or what happened after. She
thought of him and wept a little, tears shed for her own pity mostly,
the spectacle of it. Even pity has to be learned, she thought. Eddy, not
much of a weeper, listens to her go through it all again. Evening, the
local hardware store, him shuffling bolts in a drawer. Afterwards he
says some things about imagination, about hunting, but by then she
has tuned out. They return to the car. It starts again.

~~~

Don't yell. I'm not. You're hung up on your own pieties. Let's not do
this. You want to hunt without shooting. He's not an animal. You visit
him in your mind like someone going to the zoo. Can we not do this.
You're like one of those dazed women in Antonioni. Who's Anton-
ioni? Never mind. So give me the Eddy method. For sonnets? Ain't
got no sonnets in me. Not sonnets, I mean the world, the blastedness,
your work every day, the blood on the walls, the ruined people, how
do you get on with it? I define the task and complete the task. If it's
analyze the blood I analyze the blood, if it's fix the fridge door in

the lab I fix the fridge door. Define the task, complete the task. They are driving in a freezing evening now turning greenish at dusk, purple. She used to love winter, season of advent, early dark closing in, almost friendly. They stop at a stoplight. Where are we going? Your place I guess. She looks out her window at a man wrestling three enormous snowflakes out of a box onto his lawn, beside him a plastic snowman tilts on a mound of snow. Man gives her a look. The wires of his snowflakes are terribly tangled. Inside a dark house a dog is barking, barking.

barking.

~~~

You know my uncles made squirrel chowder, Eddy says. He is attaching labels to his vials. She is typing more labels. Earlier in the day they'd been out back watching a squirrel running on a wall, or trying to run. Squirrel with a bum arm. It ran along the wall, tried to turn, collapsed on the bum arm, pitched off the wall, sprang back up, tried again, pitched off again, did this a dozen times until all at once a moan of rage came out of it - the whole suffering of its squirrel life packed into one sound, calling out to gods and justice, a moan that did not stop. Eddy went back inside before she did. Five or six squirrels in a pot with some Lipton onion soup mix, few potatoes, you'd be surprised. It is beginning to bother her she can't tell when he is kidding. Do you think animals can pretend? she says. Yes but they can't pretend to pretend. What? A squirrel might deceive you as to where its stash is by running to the wrong tree if it knows you're watching. Okay. But a squirrel isn't going to run to the *right* tree to make you think it's running to the *wrong* tree and then go back later, they don't reason around corners like that. Holy crap, neither do I, she says. He looks at her. Well, she says, maybe I do. Eddy is putting vials in the transit pouch. Reminds me of a Russian joke, she says, I can't recall how it goes but the punch line is. If you say *moron* you are obviously referring to the Tsar! Eddy laughs. Why am I laughing, he says, I don't get it.

~~~

She studies photographs of Ernst Meister, who even as a young man looks like he's wearing a hairpiece. What does Ernst Meister know? Let's say you register for a doctorate the day your professor is arrested; decide to publish new drastic verse just as the Nazis denounce degeneracy; deploy to Stalingrad, get captured, imprisoned and returned from war to spend decades writing poetry no one reads. Finally, two days before your death, they all decide you're okay and award you the George Büchner Prize. Posthumously! *Zeitspalt* is a word you might use to express your thanks. "Timerift," where we dangle between nothing and nothing. Is Ernst Meister talking to her? Just fooling? What does he know? Why does it comfort her to read his "doing well for ourselves above the ash heap?" What new falsehood is this comfort, a man dead since 1979, a boy vanished in a news clip? I doubt you can hear me. I cannot shout louder than this.

~~~

~~~

Eddy is away. His lab silent. Back porch rough with leaves. It used to be possible to renounce errors, or at least name them. There is a crow on an upper branch. He moves his eye onto her.

~~~

Dangling at the yew tree, black, messy, unexhilarated, this crow, his mineral eye, his snatcher mocker self. She stares at him, makes a crow sound, four beats, he makes a crow sound, four beats, and swanks off to defend his day. She laughs. Not every crow has its eye on the George Büchner Prize. But this one, she thinks, this one might.

~~~

Eddy's birthday, an occasion his mother likes to celebrate although Eddy does not. His mother lives two hours north. She is very old, very small, very well-dressed and surprisingly avid, a bullet of a person. A sustaining member of the Country Club where a reservation has been made for 6 p.m. Bring your little friend if you like, she says to Eddy on the phone.

~~~

As they drive she looks out at March, the scraped-down hills, the thin hard light. You can almost see things coming through the back, she says. Back of what? he says. She doesn't answer. A blackness flaps by on the left. Fairly clear by now the crow *is* Ernst Meister. Eddy turns on the radio. She dozes. Wakes to a familiar sensation. But in fact she hasn't bled (monthly) for more than a year, since she started running too much and eating too little. She likes running and the power in it. But misses the feeling of a safe clean bandage between the legs after tidying oneself up. The crossover of cleanliness and filth. Odd that being with Eddy should call the blood out again, if that's what's happening, she wonders if she should tell him, a sort of tribute. She laughs. What's funny? he says. Nothing, she says. Can we stop at a rest stop?

~~~

that black bird always following you around
the crow
yes
long story
seen you feeding him
he likes toast
you're a deep well, Eddy
think so
actually no but I think you're fond of your little web of myth and
    mystery
possibly
I had a dream we were in the kitchen and I kept opening the wrong
    half of the door to the porch, the half with no screen on it and you
    got annoyed
why open the wrong half
well I guess that would be the question but
but what
but the air, the air was lovely coming in

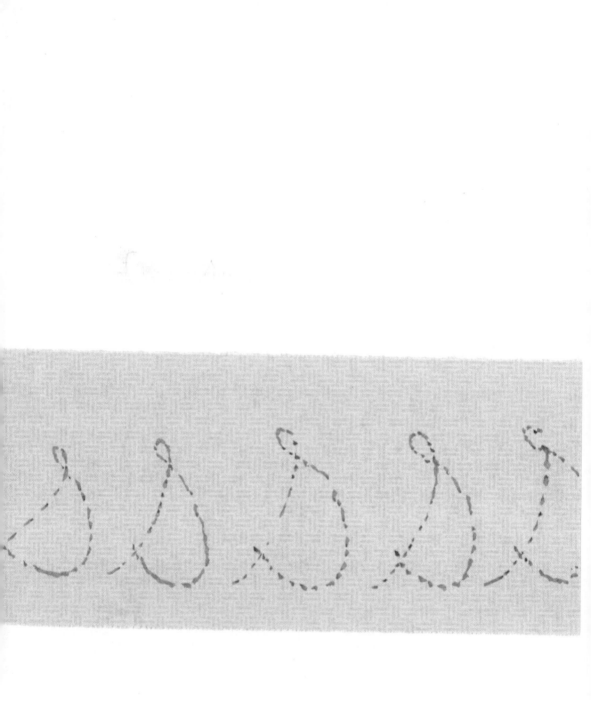

FLAUBERT AGAIN

Objects would suddenly fall or fall apart, cars go off course, dogs drop to their knees. The army was doing sound experiments at a nearby desert in those days. I was nervous all the rest of my life (she wrote). She was a novelist and enjoyed some success. But always she had the fantasy of a *different kind of novel,* and although gradually realizing that all novelists share this fantasy, she persisted in it, without knowing what it would be except true and obvious while it was happening. Now I'm *writing,* she would be able to say.

She broke off.

Where would you put a third arm? is a question asked in creativity assessment tests, or so I have heard. Will this *different kind of novel* be like that, like a third arm? I hate creativity (she said). Certainly not like a third arm. It would be less and less and less, not more. Barthes died, he never got there. She named other attempts, Flaubert, etc. Other renunciators, none of them clear on what to renounce. This chair I'm sitting in (she thought). Its fantastic wovenness, a wicker chair, old, from the back porch, brought in for winter. Me sitting here, by a lamp, wrapped in a quilt, beside the giant black windows, this December blackness, this 4.30 a.m. kitchen reflected on the glass. The glass too cold to touch. The loudness of the silence of a kitchen at night. The small creak of my chair.

To be a *different kind of novel* it would have to abolish something, abolish several things - plot, consequence, the pleasure a reader derives from answers withheld, the premeditation of these. Abolish, not just renounce them. To renounce is weak, reactive, egoistic. If she were ever really *writing* it would pull her down into itself and erase everything but her decency. She would correspond at all points to her story but her story would not be a story of heaven, hell, chaos, the world, the war at Troy or love, it would be just telling itself. It would have no gaps, no little indecent places where she didn't know what she was talking about. Because (she wanted to say) it would be a story of *nothing* and *everything* at the same time, but by now, while only dimly realizing she was more or less quoting Flaubert's famous 1852 letter about "a book about nothing" that everyone quotes when they have this idea the first time, she knew she had lost it, the murmur, the trace, the nub where it was her own and (whatever "own" means in a world where it is also "again") she was forfeit, foolish, flailing, inexact and rattling on, it had eluded her, it lets me go! I cannot bear to be let go, clenched in my quilt, a phantom receding, it rustles off, the dawn barely blueing the air, the static stopped.

Chilled and stale as the old night itself she stood up and folded the quilt, wishing she were hungry but she was not, wishing she was the kind of person who took baths but, as a rule, she did not bathe. Part of the reason for this was that at the exact moment of lowering her body into boiling hot water, for a split second, this always happens, she is five years old again and it is Sunday night and she is horrified. Horrified why? She doesn't know. School on Monday? But she did not dislike school. Or maybe she did at first. Not later. At any rate there is a rolling all-pervasive upwash of dread, one great hot shooting surge of dread-sensation through mind and body, a sense - perhaps? - of Time, carrying a body on from Sunday night to Monday morning to every Monday morning after that and on and on to extinction, this progress, this exasperating, nonnegotiable, obliterating motion forward into the dark, the dark what? And what about the sheer searing thrill of it - boiling hot bath water, this could not be denied, a brilliance shot up through it and the body fairly *sang*. Then it was gone. Is there a childhood sublime? Does it end where expectation begins? For the sublime is punctured by egotism, by the rapt, hard, small beak of my self demanding to be me. My self finding the words for that. If I can find the words I can make it real, she thought and that was when she sat down to be a writer.

At first the energy required for using her new beak obscured anxieties or questions like, What to write? and Who cares? She wrote about her friend Martha who knocked over a pile of coins in the library. She wrote about going to church with her mother-in-law on Xmas Day. She wrote about snow. It was while writing of snow, in contemplation, that doubt seeped in. And all her sentences turned their blank awful faces to her in blame. It was in the numismatics library, she wanted to say to them, but the sentences did not show pity. The same old faux-naive stuff about Martha, oh stop! they cried. Snow again! they scoffed. She went on awhile with the mother-in-law-on-Xmas-Day story anyhow, she liked that one. To comment on knees in church had seemed a bright idea, a bit of an edge.

During the sermon I crossed my legs. It worried me (she wrote). Once in Berlin she'd sat at dinner beside a man who made his living translating American crime fiction for a German publisher. Got fired. Couldn't find a non-obscene German equivalent for "she crossed her legs." Can this be true? She studied what she could see of her own legs, two knobby knees in black tights. Glancing around she saw no one else had crossed theirs. Places like church, does everyone worry? Does anyone know the rules? Were the rules discussed before I came in? Being respectful in church is a matter of impersonation. Being a daughter-in-law is too. We all impersonate people who know the rules. "I am always making myself up as I go along" (Sartre). She'd received a book on the existentialists for Xmas, people who denounced impersonation, people who said they were made nauseous by rules. She crossed her legs in the other direction. Is crossing itself the issue? Are straight lines ethically preferable to bent lines? Why do we call criminals "crooks?" She recalled studying Pythagoras in school. Early philosopher. Not existentialist. He made a list of everything in the world in two columns. He put Good, Male, Light, Limit, Straight, Accurate in one column, on the right, and Evil, Female, Dark, Unlimited, Bent, Lost in the other, on the left. There's fear in rules. Oh that Helen of Troy!

Straighten her out? Not likely! "Any man might do a girl in, any man might have to," sang Sweeney.

Sartre would have liked Sweeney. There's fear in rules and stupidity in sentences. All the old hatred of women and crookedness since Pythagoras' time having got packed down into stupid sentences, she saw it as one big grindstone grinding through days and nights and history and philosophy and novels. She thinks suddenly of Martha in the numismatics library knocking over a pile of coins. The sound was like coins, there is nothing else sounds like that being knocked over. The numismatist glared. Martha laughed later but not at the time. Her mother was in the ICU, in a city some miles away, recovering after a nine-hour surgery. Or not recovering. The doctors were obscure, the nurses overworked. Martha wished the numismatist could know this. He might have taken Martha's arm. Martha might not have wept in the stairwell.

Once she and Martha had gone to Greece together, to an international writers' conference. While they were there she'd renounced writing. Instead she made sketches in a sketchbook and titled it *The Glass of Water*, as if that's what everyone was looking for, a glass of water in Greece, not a different kind of novel or some not-stupid sentences. The sketches were a bit cartoonish but loving. We see the glass of water disappearing up the stairs with a Russian poet. Or gripped fast by a Turkish Cypriot novelist (who has poured it into two glasses). Or lost behind a mountain of toast by a Spanish writer at the breakfast table. She found toast difficult to draw convincingly, from a side view. Drawing on the Peruvian poet, on the other hand, who claimed he had videotaped his llama drinking from the glass of water, was a joy as she already knew how to draw llamas. The videotape was mostly blank. Meanwhile the former Nobel Prize winner from Ireland had seen the glass of water being hoisted (by Samuel Beckett in a bar) and "there was no pronoun for that" (he kept saying). The Serbian poet fell off the bus. He got no sympathy. He never drank water! Then finally all the writers posing after the group reading in their "owl of Athena" costumes on the last day, an indelible memory. An excellent sketch. All their crazy signatures. She and Martha had, as we say after vacations in Greece, learned a lot. They had found sharing a hotel room fairly unbearable due to their very different temperaments. It brings tears to her eyes now. She isn't sure what kind of tears they are. She opens the *Glass of Water* sketchbook to the last page. It is a drawing of empty hotel balconies. Someone has scrawled "5 a.m." on the side of the page and on the bottom "Already tomorrow is here" with a bunch of green and blue marks she can't remember making.

how do you sustain morale during a long project
Lutheran guilt
how do you sustain morale during a long project
bourbon
how do you sustain morale during a long project
just smile
how do you sustain morale during a long project
pills can help

FATE, FEDERAL COURT, MOON

The fate of the earth. The fate of me. The fate of you. The fate of Faisal. The fate of the court where Faisal will plead his case. The fate of the court's bias. Every court has a bias. It sifts to the surface gradually. The fate of whomever we drink to after court. The fate of that branch of mathematics that deals with "dead-end depth." The fate of Yemen where Faisal will probably never return. The fate of the engineering job Faisal had in Yemen before the events in question. The fate of the "simple random walk" and its difference from the "homesick random walk," concepts from a mathematics textbook I read once about dead-end depth. The fate of Montreal where Faisal lives now. The fate of his family, the ones still alive, back in Yemen, and the fate of the bridal couple, still alive, whose wedding was the target of the drone pilot (mistake). The fate of the others, not still alive (mistake). The fate of the moon that rose over us as we drove through the mountains of Pennsylvania to be present at Faisal's day in court. The fate of the silveriness of the moon that no words can ever describe. The fate of the bright sleepless night. The fate of our phones, which we decide to take to the courthouse at 9 a.m. and relinquish at the door. The fate of two guys doing a job interview in the cafeteria where we stop for coffee on the way to courtroom 31. Been around the block, says one guy. Army does the billing, says the other guy. The fate of so many men in suits and ties. The fate of being lost in marble corridors. The fate of being much too early at courtroom 31. The fate of the knot of lawyers who surround Faisal as he enters in a new suit. The fate of congratulating him on his new suit. The fate of his smile. *His smile is great.* The fate of the numerous clerks who pour glasses of water for the judges and generally fuss around. The fate of the pearls worn by Judge Tollard, who sits on the far right of the bench, which curve like teeth below her actual teeth. The fate of straining to hear what Faisal's lawyer, with his back to us, says to the judges. The fate of him perhaps saying that the government is asking the court to refrain from judging, asking the court to step back without knowing what it is stepping back from. The fate of proportionality, a matter of context. The fate of what is or is not a political question. The fate of the precedent called "al Shifa," with which everyone seems familiar. The fate of a publicly acknowledged program of targeting people who might be a danger to us.

The fate of inscrutable acronyms. The fate of me totally losing the thread of the argument as we distinguish "merits" from "standing." The fate of what Faisal is seeking, which is now given as "declaratory relief" (new phrase to me). The fate of "plaintiffs who have no chance of being harmed in the future due to being deceased," a wording that gives pause. The fate of how all this may depend on her pearls, her teeth. The fate of the words "We are really sorry, we made a mistake," which Judge Tollard utters in a hypothetical context but still it's good to hear. The fate of the government lawyer who is blonde and talks too fast, using "jurisdictional" many times and adding "as the relief sought is unavailable." The fate of wondering why it is unavailable to say "Sorry." The fate of Judge Tollard's invitation to the government lawyer to tell the plaintiff how he might "exhaust all administrative avenues of redress," as the government claims he should have done before bringing this case. "Where would he go?" Judge Tollard asks with apparent honest curiosity. "If you were he where would you go?" The fate of our bewildered conversation afterwards about why she said this, whose side she is on, what she expects Faisal's lawyers to do with it now. The fate of the tuna sandwiches eaten with Faisal while debating this. The fate of his quietness while others talk. The fate of his smile, which seems to invite the soul, centuries ago, serving tea, let's say, to guests. The moon above them. Joy. The fate of disinterestedness, of joy, of what would Kant say, of not understanding what kind of thing the law is anyway, for example in its similarity to mathematics, for they both pretend to objectivity but objectivity is a matter of wording and words can be, well, a mistake. The fate of the many thoughts that go on in Faisal when he is quiet, or the few thoughts, how would I know? The fate of the deep-sea diver that he resembles, isolated, adrift. The fate of him back in his kitchen in Montreal next week or next year, sitting on a chair or standing at the window, the moon by then perhaps a thin cry, perhaps gone. The fate of simplicity, of randomness, of homesickness, of dead ends, of souls. Who can say how silvery it was? Where would he go? Sorry?

how do you sustain morale during a long project
breathe deep
how do you sustain morale during a long project
no mirrors
how do you sustain morale during a long project
silky nightgown
how do you sustain morale during a long project
be a baby
how do you sustain morale during a long project
surrender
how do you sustain morale during a long project
frozen orange juice
how do you sustain morale during a long project
reality was a mirage interrupting me

GETAWAY

Because she has a broken heart and then her mother dies D and D take her with them on a weekend getaway. The getaway place is a honeycomb. Bees stream through the streets and the night. Bees huddling, bees zooming, bees gleaming and anxious, bees rolling along like sailors, bees licking the barley out of one another's beards. D and D are bees too and go ahead to guide her on the stream. The stream is drunk. They stumble to their rental house. I'll be fine, she thinks.

Next day they rent bikes. D and D swoop off down the bike path. She pumps the pedals hard, grinds to a halt on a dune, bruises her leg, starts again. This happens forty-five times. I haven't ridden a bike since I was ten, she explains to no one. Sweat drips down both sides of her nose. Even then Dad gave up on me. Two days down, she thinks.

On the porch in the morning a feral cat dozes at the picnic table while D eats muesli and reads aloud from *Men's Muscle* magazine. Photos of men busy transferring the insides of their bodies to the outside by pulling on chains while lightning comes from their heads. *Please, Sir, may I have another, Sir.* Others heft anvils in white shirts and ties. Reading Gogol (Nabokov observed) one's eyes become "gogolized" - people passionate about overcoats begin to appear on streets that never knew cold or snow. Will I perhaps see *mega-pec cables* romping in the rosy lanes of the honeycomb today? she wonders.

To pass the time she eavesdrops (café).
Are you tempted?
See if I lost then I'd be.
Crazy unless you're really really.
Well so, should I?
Could've said thanks but.

Can't we just be free and like this?

Difficult situation now.

Oh I know.

Never thought you felt that way.

Oh I know.

A fantasy is not a.

But I miss it like a.

And then the day ends with a churningly stupid argument between D and D in the front courtyard of a restaurant. She has a chunk of seared tuna stuck in her throat. They keep to a hiss.

You want me to be someone else.

I want you to be nothing.

That's metaphysically impossible.

Oh go away.

Years later when D and D are no longer together she wonders what it was like for them to be thugging her around behind them like an extra leg, up and down the bright boardwalks, in and out of dark shops where they tried on outfits and she wept, past terraces and bars and hooting and sex pools and other people's fly-off protocols. A night so heavy it reminds her of her mother's house, the little house by the lake where the two of them would putter in separate rooms, turning pages, thinking blazingly of one another, waiting for it to be over. Or cross paths in the kitchen and say a few words. Waiting for what to be over? The night of the seared tuna she'd returned to the rental house caked with filthy honey and lain on her back on the camp bed.

At the beach with D and D (last day) she looks down and thinks, I have her toes. She is reading only books written by people named Margaret so as to feel close to her mother. Not too close. The poor toes. In therapy (try to remember the good times) she'd come up with the one about the two of them going to the beach with no brakes on the car, her mother saying as they backed out the drive-way, *Well, it's downhill to the water and then we'll see,* and so they had. How they got home again she can't recall. They never told the father or the brother about going to the beach with no brakes, they tucked it away like some old garland from a parade at the back of the closet and glanced at it once in a while when rearranging the stuff at the front.

LECTURE ON THE HISTORY OF SKYWRITING

This is a lecture on skywriting.
Mine.
I *am* the sky.
Here follows a brief history of my life as a writer.

Preface

At first I wrote only for myself, nothing else existed. In the uncounted millennia before the big bang, when I was a riot of atmospheres and inexplicable nongravitational intensities, before the creation of galaxies or cherry trees or rational thought, before the creation of creation, I kept a few notes. I can't call it a diary because "day" as such did not yet exist but it had the same solipsistic purpose - to prevent the moments of my own life from being "allowed to waste like a tap left running," as Virginia Woolf put on p. 239 of volume I of her somewhat later contribution to the same genre. Of course "taps" as such did not yet exist either but I'm trying to give an impression of a tendency to self-reproach that I shared with Mrs. Woolf from the beginning. We writers feel the burden of being a subject-in-process no matter who we are.

Footnote 1: Linear time, a human and mortal invention, makes no sense to me, it goes without saying, insofar as I have always existed and probably will. But I recognize that humans find a temporal framework helpful in grasping larger ideas, so let's pretend that the eras of my development as a writer succeeded one another as days of the week, on a sort of Biblical model, with the modification that on the 7th day, rather than resting, I came here.

Monday.

On Monday I had innumerable girlfriends and a few boyfriends and wrote up lists of these with capsule biographies and ratings on a scale of 1 to 10. Also a fair number of sonnets. The universe was expanding, redshift by redshift. Most of my paramours were chunks of frozen rock - miniature suns, minor moons, dwarf planets. I struggled with a few passionate asteroids but in general avoided asteroids as being too small to get hold of. I was a superhot superdense young sky and I liked a good bit of rebound, especially against the cosmic microwave background of that first day of my, so to speak, autobiographical week. It was a rubbery time, nothing was nailed down, emotions oscillated like crazy, every desire broke me open in a dawn of Tiepolo pink - yet I have to say, I was never more physically fit. Due to the level of g-force pressure experienced during cosmogonic workouts, I could chart hourly improvements in bone density, lymphatic drainage and overall mood. Sex was my angel of reality on Monday, better than bowling or daily aspirin. I didn't worry about being exhausted by Tuesday. But then, late Monday night, a certain Alkmene broke my heart and I had to pause.

Alkmene was a nymph of Argos with light-brown hair. She was unusually tall. I'm speaking metaphorically, there were no nymphs or light-brown hair or tall or short at the time: there was hydrogen, there was helium, there were nuclei interreacting in an atmosphere of persistent radio noise at a temperature slightly above absolute zero ($-273°$ C). But a nymph makes a good story and, given the pace of activity on Monday, I had to fall back on narrative cliché.

So, during that era of my unbridled panspermia and serial fireball fusions, I was coupling with nymphs and engendering heavy elements all over the universe. I kept a list, as I said, and Alkmene was number 1,408. 1 saw no reason why my 1,408th nuclear interreaction should be any different than the previous 1,407 but there you go, the heart has its reasons which reason knoweth not, as someone said (Pascal). I liked Alkmene much too much. She liked me not at all. Technically she was already married - had stopped expanding her galaxies - but I was undaunted. She told me she found me "an inelegant solution to a nonessential problem." And in fact, the night I had my way with her she went immediately down the hall and slept with her husband. The result of this 3-angled sex act was Herakles, a creature in whom matter decoupled from light. Born with a 2-fold nature, half mortal and half immortal - not a single incandescent clarity existing everywhere at once without regret like me - Herakles was a thing of ordinary substance, a thing with specific life and limits in space and time. In other words he had to die.

Christopher Hitchens once said to me that having a child is like your own heart walking around in another body. So there went my own heart walking towards its own death, every millennium, every hour closer. I could not bear this. I decided to make a deal with the laws of physics, or maybe it was the laws of metaphysics, I get those two confused, anyway we all agreed that if Herakles were to set himself on fire and burn to death, his finite human nature could be purged away in the flames and leave the infinite part, the part like me. I thought this a clever solution. Unfortunately I overlooked the essence of death as an event: it happens in time. For a mortal creature death is instantaneous - you're alive one minute, dead the next. But for a creature who exists (like myself) outside time, death has no instant. I have no instant. I am *at all times*. I have to watch my most beloved child burn to death *at all times*. And I always will.

Monday is the day I learned not to make deals with the system.

Tuesday.

Tuesday I became clouds. Possibly a defensive measure - everyone loves clouds, they lift the heart, they lift the eye. Actually they lift the heart *because* they lift the eye. Cognitive scientists say that people place gods in the high blue sky because looking up causes a rush of dopamine in the brain. Yet clouds do more than draw your eye upwards. They invent your imagination.

This happens on a small scale when you lie on your back on a hill on a summer day gazing up and saying, Oh look that one's a camel! there's Werner Herzog! a can opener! the Taj Mahal! - the interpretation and reinterpretation of shifting shapes of cloud is one of the most basic exercises in free imagining known to you dwellers on the earth; also useful for reminding you that most of the ideas you conceive about the world are fragmentary, fugitive, self-ruining and soon forgotten. However, when *I* talk, within the framework of my autobiography as a writer, about inventing the imagination, I mean something else.

For a while during the so-called Enlightenment era, when human beings in general, especially highbrow middle-class Europeans, were so gripped by rationalism and so besotted with notions of intellectual control that natural science lectures offered on topics from hydraulics, magnetics and mathematics to volcanoes and the operations of the human heart were attended by hundreds of people, during that (as I say) tender-minded era, I made myself available to analysis. I gave them to believe that I, the clouds, could be reduced to a typology.

It was hard work. I had to replace the shapeless caprice of my atmospheres with 4 basic cloud types. I had to edit the indecipherably fluid filigree of my language into a dry-as-dust classificatory system replete with Latin terminology. And beyond that, I had to be flirtatious. If you bring a concept or category up close enough to the human mind to be *very very* attractive and then whisk it away so it stays out of reach, it becomes erotic. Flirting is not in my nature but who would be bothered doing science if it weren't erotic.

The 4 basic cloud types, as defined by amateur nephologist Mr. Luke Howard in a lecture at Plough Court in London on 10th December 1802, are: cirrus, cumulus, stratus and nimbus. Cirrus, from the Latin for "lock of hair," means a tendril or fibrous shape; cumulus from the Latin for "heap" or "pile" means a heap or pile; stratus from the Latin for "layer" means a horizontal band; and nimbus, Latin "cloud," is a rainy combination of the 3 previous types. It was, let me repeat, hard work to dash about the universe impersonating these 4 cloud formations, not to mention the ceaseless transitions between them with their seductive lacy gaps, and to keep this up day and night for years until Mr. Luke Howard gathered enough data for his taxonomy. It was an athletic time for me, I had to practice a lot and the tricky thing about practicing if you're the sky is there's nowhere to go to be alone; you are already everywhere. I won't burden you with the solution I found for this, it involves string theory and we haven't got to that day of the week yet.

Mr. Luke Howard's taxonomy of clouds was just one small component of the scientization of all things that began with Descartes and has shaped the mess in which the present world finds itself; still, I am perversely proud to have been a part of it, insofar as my contribution was a work of fiction and ought to have subverted the whole tax-onomical process. I admit I was surprised when Reason prevailed. And from this I learned never to be surprised when Reason prevails, especially if its data are imaginary. At the same time, the experience refreshed and refocused my own creative process. Let me quote here John Cage: "Something has to be done to get us free of our memories and choices."

Wednesday.

Exhausted with hauling myself around the upper air in cloud masquerade, I decided on Wednesday to sit at my desk, use the telephone and do an interview. I interviewed pebbles and small rocks. Insofar as I have (so to speak) all the time in the world, I could interview all the pebbles and small rocks in the world simultaneously. Even so it was a quiet experience. The questions were formulated as a sort of quiz. Here's a precis of the most interesting answers that the pebbles and small rocks gave to my questions.

1. smoothness
2. the Krumbein phi scale of sedimentology
3. Mars
4. golf on Mars
5. put up signs expressing state of mind, e.g., Yes! I love you! Help!

My questions had been concerned with the following areas, respectively:

1. criteria for racial or class prejudice in your community
2. a better way to judge the National Book Awards
3. favourite vacation spot
4. favourite vacation activity
5. what you would do first if you had hands

Well, the pebbles and small rocks interview didn't even take all morning so after lunch I picked up the phone again and called that gentleman everyone was waiting for in the latter part of the 20th century. Here is a transcription of our chat:

First things first, do I call you *Go*dot or Go*dot*?
Why not use my first name.
Okay, what's that?
Rusty.
So tell me, Rusty, how did it all get started, the non-arriving?
Started in a thinness.
What sort of thinness?
Thinness like that plate you climb back up over from behind when waking from a very flat dream.
Any narrative trajectory?
To keep moving at all times and avoid touching the hole at the centre of the thinness.
What's the hole for?
To discourage snooping.
Any music?
A sort of honkytonk thing, mostly percussion, I didn't like it, I didn't do the music.
What about lighting?
Floodlights.
Oh Rusty, how exhausting.
Yes exhausting. Not to say boring. I would have been monumentally bored had I not met Yoko Ono who gave me several suggestions for passing the time.
Like for example?
Like for example, send a note of appreciation to silent courageous people you bump into - metalworkers, mothers, street sweepers, etc. Keep doing it. See what happens.
That might be a good note to end on. Faintly redemptive.
Oh but listen, I have quite a few anecdotes left.

You know, Rusty, it's been a hard morning for me.

How so, Mr. Sky?

I been trying to get a few sound bites out of the pebbles and small rocks.

Ah the pebbles and small rocks. Say no more.

You know them?

He auditioned a lot of pebbles and small rocks before he hired me.

One can see why.

Oh sure. Good looks, natural talent. But no method, no sense of elsewhere. Pebbles and small rocks don't know how to bring it up from inside.

Did you enjoy working with him?

God no, what a monster. If we asked him questions about the text he'd warn us to be on guard against "committing reason."

Sounds like John Cage.

Oh much harsher man than Cage. "Build a little kingdom then shit on it," he would say.

I am familiar with that impulse.

Well, time for my afternoon nap, goodbye Mr. Sky.

Thank you, Rusty, it has been a consoling hour.

Thursday.

Maybe because Wednesday had been a good day, almost Proustian, I made the mistake on Thursday of attempting to write a memoir of childhood and all but vanished into its vortex of prehistoric pain. There were mountains piled on mountains, mothers frustrated, fathers castrated, brothers and sisters driven down to hell, the usual family horror and disputes about who gets to use the car - I won't bore you. I drew a big X through the manuscript, deleted it from the computer and sent a note to Yoko Ono.

Footnote 2: Memoir writing was for me a process that entailed long periods of silent reflection during which I tried to keep my mind motionless and my eyes downcast. Here is my favourite thing to look at with eyes downcast:

Forest shade, lake shade, poplar shade, highway shade, backyard shade, café shade, down behind the high school shade, cow shade, carport shade, blowing shade, dappled shade, shade darkened by rain above, shade under ships, shade along banks of snow, shade beneath the one tree in a bright place, shade by the ice-cream truck, shade in the new car salesroom, shade in halls of the palace as all the electric lights turn on, shade in a stairwell, shade in tea barrels, shade in books, shade of clouds running over a distant landscape, shade on bales in the barn, shade in the pantry, shade in the icehouse (the smell of shade), shade under runner blades, shade along branches, shade at night (a difficult research), shade on rungs of a ladder, shade on pats of butter sculpted to look like scallop shells, shade to holler from, shade in the chill of bamboo, shade at the core of an apple, confessional shade, shade of hair salons, shade in a joke, shade in the town hall, shade descending from legendary ancient hills, shade under the jaws of a dog with a bird in its mouth trotting along to the master's voice, shade at the back of the choir, shade in pleats, shade clinging to arrows in the quiver, shade in scars.

Footnote 3: Meditating on shade led me to ponder absent presence in general and to begin to worry about those many sky-related questions which will undoubtedly remain unanswered when this lecture is finished.

1. Is the sky blue.
2. Is the sky round.

3. Is it proper to use the informal 2nd-person singular pronoun *tu* or *toi* when addressing the sky.

4. Do hawks and falcons look so fantastic rising and falling because they have the sky as background or would they look equally good flying through mud or a piece of corduroy.

5. Ontologically speaking, is the sky *something* or merely what is left over because everything else has edges.

6. Can the sky break.

    a) If it broke could it be built again.

    b) If built again would it change its ways.

7. Is there one sky or many.

    a) If many, do they know about each other or wonder.

8. Are there some outcast skies.

9. Is it true the question mark derives from the shape of the tail of a cat when surprised. Sorry unfair question. Here's another: if a scholar of the Rig Veda went to a Chinese restaurant what would his fortune cookie say. Answer: CONGRATULATIONS YOU LOVE CHINESE FOOD.

Footnote 4: Now that we're so well embarked on footnotes, which have their own sort of sluggish energy, here's four minutes of deleted material from Wednesday's interview with Rusty:

What did your father do?
Cows.
How many cows?
Five or six.
Did you help with the cows?
Yes every day down to the river we went.
What were those days like?
Long.
What did you do?
I talked to them.

Talked to the cows.

No, mostly to the plants, I studied all the plants, tasted all the plants, talked to all the plants and introduced them to one another.

Why talk to the plants not to the cows?

Plants know how to listen, cows don't, cows are crazy especially ours, ours never got enough to eat, people think cows are fat and peaceful but those are government cows, the government buses those cows ahead to anywhere there's going to be photo ops, those are the cows that show up on TV living the good life. But ours were scrawny and terrible and ran all over the place.

Still, the cow-herding days must have been good training for you, for the non-arriving.

I guess.

Seems to me that, although waiting is hard, especially waiting for something that never arrives, never arriving is hard too and has just about as much waiting in it.

Well, I've got a talent for it.

Me too actually, being the sky involves a fair amount of just hanging there.

Oh it's very different.

Different how?

Well, one thing, I have to keep out of sight, but then also, and this is a factor very few people appreciate about my work, non-arriving isn't one big simple thing, it's different every time, every case unique, it's tricky, layered, psychological work - analogies like web and maze come to mind - a long, painful, undirected intimacy between strangers with no common goal. Ideally I make a slow appeal to feelings unexpressed and end by drawing tears from the stone.

Sounds like the secret police.

And there's a pissload of research gone into all this - I have a non-arrival typology I could share.

Spare me.

Maybe later.

But here's a question I've been curious about for years, Rusty, never knew how to frame it, I still hesitate.

Let's have it.

Why do you never arrive - oh I know it's your job, your assignment, your role in the play but tell me the truth, isn't there something deeper going on?

Like what?

Like bearing witness to the atrocities of our time.

Nope.

Really.

Never gave a fart for atrocities.

You're not calling history to account, you're not using silence to speak louder than words and put us all in the rearview mirror of our mean and ending world?

Nope.

And we should draw no apocalyptic conclusions whatso-ever from your steely reticence?

You know what, every October I rake apocalyptic conclu-sions into a pile in the backyard and burn them.

Do you.

But I suspect we've lost track of your original question.

Which was, *why don't you arrive?*

Why don't I arrive.

Yes.

Okay I'll give you an answer but you won't like it and you'll say we can't end there.

Shoot.

Who told me this was my Uncle Roy, I liked Uncle Roy, a little short man full of fantastic alibis, he worked for the State Dept. a long time then made a fortune by inventing the You Are Here *map for public places, you know that big map they have in parks and metro stops, and the thing about* You Are Here *maps is, by the time it's been up a year or year and a half the* You *is entirely rubbed off.*

No kidding.

So says Uncle Roy.

They rub it right off.

Because everybody wants to touch the You *when they're lost.*

Ah.

And it has to be painted back on. That's one guy's entire job all day to go around repainting second-person pronouns on You Are Here *maps.*

What about the red dot.

Well the fact is, the red dot doesn't usually disappear, it's just the You.

Haunting.

No, it's a different kind of paint.

Ah.

So let me do a question now.

Okay.

How do you think the interview went?

Our interview?

Yes. You're the expert, I'm just an amateur. And I like to know how other people go about their craft.

Well, to be honest, Rusty, I was a little disappointed in my own performance, in the sense that, whenever I listen to interviews on the radio, they get in at least once and usually several times the question, *And how did that make you feel?* but with you I didn't find any place to work it in.

Hmmm. Tell you what, I'll ask you *that question.*

Just out of the blue?

No, I'll give you a context. Here, let's say it's dusk in America, you're not the Sky anymore you're some travelling salesman driving along the freeway and you pass one of those suburban, what do you call it, housing developments with a lot of little houses all the same and a big billboard that says, If you were here you'd already be home, *how does that make you feel?*

Wow, Rusty, what a great question, I have to think about that one.

Take your time.

Well, hmmm, it makes me sad then happy, happy then sad, and here I'll quote Proust who was, with that weird devious moral power of his, able to capture in words so perfectly this quintessential experience of all the creeping creatures that creep upon the earth: *And so it was from the Guermantes way that I learned to distinguish those states of mind that follow one another in me, during certain periods, and that even go so far as to divide up each day among them, one returning to drive away the other, with the punctuality of a fever; contiguous, but so exterior to one another, so lacking in means of communication among them, that I can no longer understand, no longer even picture to myself in the one what I desired or feared or accomplished in the other.* That was *Swann's Way* translated by Lydia Davis.

I like it.

Me too.

Friday.

On Friday I decided to delegate. Why do all this thankless work writing if I can hire a ghost? So for a while I experimented with skywriters, sky-typers and sky-dot-matrix printers: there are aeronautical experts who perform all these media in little aeroplanes that exude picturesque white smoke. I have to say I was disappointed in the level of invention overall. I had envisioned epic poems in hexameter verse arcing across the heavens from Patagonia to Paris, not "I LOVE YOU DORIS" and ads for Lucky Strike. Capitalism got its hooks into this art form from its first breath in 1922. But halfway through Friday I realized I was on the wrong track. I was looking to the public for what could only be private. I had to step back from the marketplace to the inside of the mind. That's when I became a Hindu. Or at least very deeply interested in what Hindu scholars of the Rig Veda mean by *writing*.

The hymns of the Rig Veda contain the following suggestion: "Something only exists if consciousness perceives it as existing. And if a consciousness perceives it, within this consciousness there must be another consciousness perceiving the consciousness that perceives," and so forth. You can pursue this regress in an inward direction, as Vedic scholars do, or you can go the other way and find sky upon sky upon sky perceiving all the degrees of consciousness in the cosmos. You need to take a breath to think this. And your breath *is* the thinking. We think each other back and forth, your mind and me. We write one another.

Put this a different way: consciousness and sky, or mind and cosmos, are organically related. They mirror and enact one another. The Vedic scholars whose care was to transmit the thousands of hymns and ritual directives and meditations that comprise the Rig Veda did so for 3 millennia by oral tradition, without writing down a single word, because they saw the texts inscribed inside their minds. Of course they had to pay attention. And for the most part they were fantastically scrupulous, both in reading these inward texts and in performing the rituals prescribed by them. But a wonderful and forgiving aspect of Hindu thought, to me at least, is the notion they had that, if someone did make a mistake in a ritual, a witness who noticed the error and who knew the correct text could mend the mistake on the sky of his mind and so make the cosmos perfect again, microphysically.

I spent the rest of Friday noticing various acts of mending going on throughout the cosmos here and there. I felt calm

and hopeful. Then about 12 o'clock my mood changed,
I'm not sure why, it was midnight but darker.

قمت اليوم من النوم وأنا مجغور ، قد ظهر لي وأنا اتحاكا هانا من
منبع سيرتي الذاتية ـ أن عتباقي مساحة كبيرة من تجربتي الشخصية
عادني ماقد ذكرتهاش . وانا قصدي أن سماء هذه الأرض قد سارت
وسيلة لنقل أسلحة الموت والقتل لأهلها. الحرب هي واحدة من حقائق
الحياة لكل المخلوقات الذي تحبي على وجه الارض (مثلما وصفها
سفر التكوين في اليوم السادس الأخير من خلق السموات والأرض).
والحرب في الغالب تاريخ ممتد من أدوات للقتل وسفك الدماء تتطاير
عبر الأثير وما بش فرق من حيث النتيجة بين رصاص البنادق
والقنابل وبين السهام والنبال أو بين هذه وبين مدافع الموت الذي
طورها الالمان في الحرب العالمية الثانية , والمعروفة باسم بيق
برثا أو قاذفة القنابل البعيدة المدى الأمريكية المعروفة باسم بي
فيفتني تو . أو مقذوفات الغازات السامة والصواريخ النووية العابرة
للحدود أو بين هذه وبين مقذوفات المنجنيق من الحجارة أو كرات
النار الملتهبة و الطائرات المسيرة المميتة كلها على اختلاف
عصرها ومدى قوتها على القتل، ادوات لهادم اللذات ومفرق
الجماعات. كل هذا خلاني اتفيضل في كتابة ماعندي علاسب أبدع
في صياغة هذه التأملات في رواية من روايات الجريمة السريعة
الإيقاع، وبالفعل فقد حصلت جرائم حرب.

ولكن ظهر لي بعدها انه مستحيل اختصار هذا الطريق الطويل
من شرور البشر في معادلة رياضية بسيطة عن أسباب جرائم
الحرب وآثارها. كما تتسم روايات الجريمة الخيالية بدرجة عالية
من التكثيف وتأثيرها على القارئ يأتي من خلال الوجه الذي ترسمه
لعناصر وشخوص القصة أي الضحية والجلاد والمحقق أو رجل
البوليس السري فلكل هؤلاء من الخيرين أو الاشرار وجه معروف
به. أما الحروب وعبر تاريخها فقد شهدت تطور كبيرا لتسير مع
مرور الوقت بلا وجه. واكيد أن هيكتور و اقلاسيس بسروا إلى
اعين بعضهما البعض في ميدان الحرب , إلا أنه في عام 1092 وجد
البابا أوربان الثاني أنه من الضروري تجريم آلة إطلاق السهام و
النبال لكونها شوعة علاسب أنها تقتل من بعيد (يعني مابش
مواجهة), وفي القرن الحادي و العشرين يستر جندي في مدينة نيفادا
أن يهمس زرا واحدا ويقتل خمسة أشخاص في باكستان و يحرقهم
حتى يوقعوا دخانا.

'اذا ما بش وجه ,ماعد عيوقعش هاناك أخلاقيات, هذه فكرة قديمة. ولكن ايضا بدون الوجه (ماعيوقعليش) مهرة و لا حاجة لأكتب عنها. فلا تستر تكتب جملة واضحة و مفهومة باستعمال الأفعال بس . ولا تستر تحكي قصة بدون ان تؤمن بحقيقة وجود بني آدم آخرين.

إلى الان ماقد تنبأتش ان كل هذه المخلوقات التافهة الذي تمشي على الأرض عاتتوقف رغبتها في الحرب في أي زمان او وقت قريب وماقد توقعتش أنا نفسي ان اتوقف عن نقل رغباتكم الهيستيرية في عشيقاتكم الحروب عبر هواء السماء الزرقاء.

هذا ما ًخلقنا عليه. والسبت كان هو اليوم الذي اعترفت فيه بهذا.

Saturday.

Saturday I awoke conflicted. For I realized, autobiographically speaking, that there remained one vast area of self-experience as yet unexplored and unexplained, viz. *sky as a medium of annihilation*. Warfare is a fact of life for all the creeping creatures that creep upon the earth (as the book of Genesis calls them on the 6th day) and warfare is mostly a history of death-bringing stuff flying through the air - bullets, bombs, bows and arrows, Big Berthas, B-52s, poison darts, poison gas, portable nukes, cannonballs, curses, lethal drones. My first instinct was to fashion all this into a fast-paced crime novel. Certainly there were crimes.

But it proved impossible to condense that long evildoing into a simple algebra of cause and effect. Crime fiction is very condensed. And its impact on the reader derives from giving *a face* to the algebraic components - the victim, the criminal, the detective, the good, the bad. Warfare has grown increasingly faceless throughout its history. Surely Hektor and Akhilles looked into each other's eyes on the battlefield, but in 1092 Pope Urban II found it necessary to outlaw the crossbow as being inglorious due to its distance from death, and by the 21st century a soldier in Nevada can push a button and have five people in Pakistan burst into flame. Without the face, no ethics: this is an old idea. But also, without the face, no function for me, nothing to write about. No one can make sentences using only verbs. No one can tell a story without believing in the reality of others.

Yet I didn't, I don't, expect all you creeping creatures that creep upon the earth to stop wanting warfare anytime soon. And I didn't, I don't, expect me to stop delivering the hysterical valentines of your desire through my beautiful blue air.

That's who we are.

Saturday was the day to acknowledge this.

Every writer's week arrives at a Saturday, a day when he wishes it were Monday again and he could start over with the innocence of his first sonnets. Or even the relative rectitude of Tuesday, when the Enlightenment was dawning and Immanuel Kant was writing sentences like, "Two things move me to wonder: the starry sky above me and the moral law within me." Those starry skies don't come back.

So now it is **Sunday.**
Creation rests. I close my notes. Like every author, when I come to the end of a piece of writing, it is quite clear to me that I will never write again. The upper air, the middle air, the lower air, is blank. Blankness plunges out of it. Blankness plunges out of it and goes elsewhere. And, I suppose, it will arrive.

how do you sustain morale during a long project
dress dandy
how do you sustain morale during a long project
I love you
how do you sustain morale during a long project
yes
how do you sustain morale during a long project
I don't know
how do you sustain morale during a long project
not a fan
how do you sustain morale during a long project

LITTLE RACKET

Sunday evening, grey on grey. All day the storm did not quite storm. Clouds closed in, sulked and spat. We put off swimming. Took in the chairs. Finally (about seven) a rumbling high up. A wind swept the trees, tossing each once, releasing rivulets of cool air downward and this wind which came apart on the wind, the parts swaying, descending, bumping around the yard awhile not quite rain until a single sudden chord ran drenched across the roof, the porch and - stopped. We breathed. Maybe that's it. Maybe it's over, the weatherman is often wrong these days, we can still go swimming (glimpse of sun?) when all at once the sluices opened, broke a knot and smashed the sky to bits and it fell and keeps falling even now as dark comes on and fabled Night is managing its manes and the birds, I can hear from their little racket, the birds are burning up and down like holy fools somewhere inside it - far inside there where they keep the victim, smeared, stinking - hence the pageantry, hence the pitchy cries, *don't keep saying you don't hear it too.*

what is your philosophy of time
I feel like in a giant chestnut
what is your philosophy of time
I'm quite sure we'll surrender
what is your philosophy of time
how it's sweet and how it moves
what is your philosophy of time
it is a way to travel
what is your philosophy of time
a shallow closet with narrow bench and a rope to pull you up
what is your philosophy of time
thin cradle of feathers

do you like the films of Eric Rohmer
sexy
do you like the films of Eric Rohmer
very much
do you like the films of Eric Rohmer
no idea
do you like the films of Eric Rohmer
do you like jam
I do

MEXICO!

It was the corner we came round from the highway on the way back from visiting Dad, last corner before the turn-off. Greyish-brown corner, greyish-brown November, so I remember but was it always November? - he stayed in that facility for years - those few thin grasses straggling for life at the place where three roads met in a smear of raw snow, the unbeautiful trees poking up from a ditch on either side. Crack the window, you'd smell root, ash, needle, cold. Memory is a novelist, it saturates the data with its own toxins. Bleakness seizes me when I think of rounding that corner on a November afternoon and the other parts of day, before and after, the morning and the evening, leaking out of it on either side, the lives of us leaking out of it. Turning onto our own road meant goodbye transit time, no more self suspended, no more streaming along as a person in a car on the way to some-where else. We went by taxi, neither she nor I drove (Dad used to drive). Her up front with the taxi driver, me in back keeping close to the window, watching the land-scape, me looking out. Me thinking of myself looking out, then of other things, lunch, Christmas, an artwork I heard about once called *Horses Endlessly Running*. It was a miniature chessboard and all the pieces were knights - was it in Mexico? - yes I looked it up, it was Mexico (Gabriel Orozco) and *Mexico!* came to me like an alteration of death to life, just the word, just the thought, the little hooves drumming across the dwarf chessboard, the small hearts storming the small hot breasts, the tiny forelocks and fetlocks and withers bright with the dew of a small-scale dawn - yes it was Mexico and all the pieces were knights! All the pieces were endlessly, gallantly, blessedly, blythesomely knights.

do you like the films of Eric Rohmer
love in the afternoon is fantastic
do you like jam
yes when in need
do you like jam
nothing swampy please
do you like the films of Eric Rohmer
too sugary
do you like jam
I like watching paint dry

OH WHAT A NIGHT
(a translation of Alkibiades's speech from Plato's *Symposium*)

Plato's *Symposium*: Prelude

A symposium was usually a gentleman's drinking party. This is an unusual one. It has been going on for hours with no drinking. The participants agreed at the outset to forego wine in favour of entertaining one another with speeches in praise of love. Phaidros, Pausanias, Eryximachos, Aristophanes and Agathon have spoken; Sokrates is just subsiding to applause when a knock comes at the door. Alkibiades blunders in, very loud, very drunk and covered in garlands. Boisterous confusion follows. When they catch sight of one another Alkibiades and Sokrates engage in a mock display of lovers' jealousy (or maybe it's real). Alkibiades proclaims that everyone should at once get as drunk as he is. He insists on contributing a symposiastic speech, not in praise of love but in praise of Sokrates. He drapes his garlands over Sokrates and begins.

My praise of Sokrates, here goes:
Begin with a likeness -
just to give you a mental image.
(Images are true):

that Silenus doll
they sell in the shops,
you know the one,
you can crack it in two

and surprisingly inside are
little figures of gods -
he's like that. He's a bit like
Marsyas the satyr too.

He has Marsyas' lips
except Marsyas puts his lips
to his flute to
ravish you.

Sokrates just talks.

Talk here is common.
In Athens orators are hot - Perikles for instance.
Now Perikles is good, but

listening to him can be pretty predictable.
When Sokrates speaks, on the other hand,
I experience something uncanny,
I don't know what

it is - a wild feeling
like a heart attack, or like dancing -
those nights you dance as if in a trance
and glance in the mirror to find you're in tears.

I'm not drunk.
This is different.
I know it sounds
like the same old same old,

but that man can carry you off your head.
His talk made me weep.
I ran from him.
I can't live that way,

He tells me (which is true) that
my values are all wrong: I'm just a crowd-pleaser.
He says my whole life
is papier-mâché.

Well, I don't want to sit by this siren till I die of old age.
So what's the reason I can't turn the page?
Simple answer. Shame.
He's the only man in the world who can see through my game.

Yet the fact is, if he were to
from the world vanish,
my heart would
famish.

Let's go back
to my original analogy:
Sokrates
as satyr.

He likes beautiful men, as everyone knows.
Near them he lights up, he goes fizzing
round the room
like a carbonated vapour.

At the same time
he claims to know nothing,
be ignorant,
empty, the opposite of wise.

It's a pretty good disguise.
But crack him open -
you find something utterly different inside -
not like gold, not like god,

not like any other beauty -
I glimpsed it once.
And after that I
had to do everything he said.

But my calculation was, say
he's seriously hot for my looks and my charm -
all I do is gratify him,
he'll tell me everything in his head.

Such was my view of my looks and my charm.
I sent everyone away and met him one to one.
(Sokrates, speak up
if I'm getting any of this wrong.)

I was assuming, you see, we'd immediately fall into
one of those special conversations lovers have when alone.
Well, nothing happened.
He conversed as usual. At the end of the day went home.

I took him to the gym.
We worked out.
Wrestled.
All alone.

Nothing happened.
Sokrates 2 Alkibiades 0,
I said to me.
So I stopped being coy,

asked him to dinner.
Hmmm, he said but eventually, reluctantly agreed -
as if I were the lover and he
the sought-after boy!

The first time he came, he just ate and left.
The second time, I had a ploy.
Kept him talking far
into the night.

When he rose to go I said,
It's late,
you're tired,
no doubt a bit tight,

just stay. He lay down on the little bed by my side.
Now the next part of this
I would not confide
except I'm

A: drunk
B: too honest to stop
C: like one of those snakebitten people
who can only talk about snakebite.

But of course this is worse -
I've been bitten in my heart or my soul or whatever we call it -
by the philosophic words of this man:
those words can zero in.

They strike, they wound, they go
deep
in the system,
I've a very tender system.

And those words make me do
whatever they want.
But now, looking round this room
I see

pretty much all of you've shared in the -
should I say crazy? should I say sublime?
experience
of Sokrates' philosophy:

Agathon, Phaidros,
Eryximachos, Pausanias,
Aristodemos,
Aristophanes -

if I tell you
what I did and what I said,
gentlemen,
give me your sympathy, please.

Going back to that night:
the lamp was out, the slaves withdrawn.
No point being subtle, I thought. Just say it.
I shook him.

"You asleep?"
"Why, no."
"Tell you what I've decided."
"Okay, shoot."

"You, in my view, Sokrates,
are the only worthy lover I've had.
But you're shy to get anything going.
Here's my position:

failing to gratify you would be folly on my part.
This [gestures to self]
or anything else you need - my wealth, my friends -
it's yours. I have one goal: for me

to be the best Alkibiades I can be.
You could help. Better than anyone else.
I'd be ashamed *not* to give a man like you
whatever he wants."

At this Sokrates, in his usual ironic manner,
said, "Alkibiades darling,
you're no fool after all
if you see in me some power to make you better.

It must be a kind of beauty vastly different to your own,
a rare, an extraordinary kind -
so what you're proposing
is an exchange of beauty for beauty?

Now is that a fair deal? Your beauty for mine? Alleged for true?
Sounds like the same old bargain of bronze for gold."
Then he warned me off dealmaking in general,
said something else about the eyes of the soul,

and that was that.
I declared I'd made my feelings clear
and now it was up to him.
He said okay.

I'd shot my bolt, so to say.
Pretty sure I'd scored a hit.
So I got up, threw my coat over us - it was winter -
crawled under his cloak and wrapped my arms around this miraculous man.

And we lay that way all night long.
(Sokrates, speak up if I tell a lie.)
Now you, gentlemen of the jury, I put it to you:
did he not flout me, disdain me, make mock of my looks and my charm?

Don't you call that insulting?
For I swear by the gods and all the goddesses,
when I rose in the morning I had no more *slept with Sokrates*
than if I'd lain with my father or brother.

You can imagine what a state I was in.
Affronted yes, but marvelling
at the self-control of the man!
His inner strength, his integrity are like no other.

So I didn't want to act hysterical and lose him,
but I had no idea
how to seduce him.
Money, I knew, was not his interest.

And I'd already played
what I thought was my ace (the looks and the charm).
I was baffled, bedazzled, didn't know what to do.
Then we got called up: winter is

not a good time to go to war.
Potidaia,
the siege,
we bivouacked together.

Well, first of all, hardship was nothing to him.
He could go without food,
he could drink us all under the table.
But his attitude to cold weather

amazed us most - winters there are fierce: one time
we had a frost so cold no one would leave the tent,
or else they'd put on all their clothes
and wrap their feet in felt and fleece.

This man went out in his usual shirtsleeves,
no shoes at all,
and crossed the ice
without fuss.

The others looked askance at him.
He was "mighty of heart"
like a hero in Homer.
He worried them.

Here's another example.
Early one day he was struck by a thought
and stood from dawn in the same spot,
pondering.

He just couldn't get it,
continued to stand, continued to ponder.
Noon came on.
The others were noticing.

"Sokrates has stood in the same place since dawn,"
said one to another,
"thinking something."
It was a notably hot summer day.

At evening some took their bedding outside
and watched him to see if he'd stand there all night.
He stood there all night.
And at dawn, after offering a prayer to the sun, he went his way.

Here's another. This is a good one.
Was the day I got my medal of honour
from the generals.
To this man here, no one else, I owe thanks

for saving my life.
I was wounded. He refused to leave.
He got me and my weapons off the field intact.
I urged everyone in the higher ranks

to give you the medal that day,
Sokrates, you know this is true.
You cannot rebuke me.
You waved it away.

And then the battle of Delium,
the big retreat.
I was on horseback, Sokrates on the ground.
He was marching beside another man,

totally calm, completely unflustered -
in fact, to steal a phrase of yours,
Aristophanes,
if I can,

he was "swaggering along like a kingfisher bird,"
tossing a glance from side to side,
making quite clear he was not one to mess with.
Of course he and his comrade got home just fine.

That's a lesson of war:
act cool, no one lays a finger on you.
Ah, so many lessons, so many stories
if I had time.

So many great men to compare him to.
Perikles! Akhilles! Nestor! all those
celebrated heroes of the present and the past -
but no.

No one is like this.
His strange way of being.
His strange way of talking.
There is no likeness.

At least not among humans.
Let's go back
to my original analogy:
Satyrs and Silenuses.

What I forgot to say before -
his language cracks open
just like those dolls.
At first everything he says

sounds a little bizarre:
it's all donkeys and cobblers and men who tan leather,
ever the same examples,
ever the same jargon.

But look inside!
They open up
into something astonishing!
Call it a god, or moral perfection,
or an inexplicable pure gold bargain -

his are the only words that make sense!
And that, gentlemen, is my praise of Sokrates.
I mixed it up with a bit of blame.
He did after all insult my pride.

For we all know a lover and his
boy are not interchangeable.
Yet Sokrates acts as if *he* were the boy dazzler
and *I* the old guy begging for love.

He's done the same
to any number of others.
Agathon, watch out.
I don't want to say he's a hustler.

I don't want to say you're a fool.
But recall what they told us at school:
by suffering we learn.
Now it's your turn.

Symposium: Postlude

So Alkibiades ends his speech. There is laughter from the others, who perceive him to be still very much besotted with Sokrates. Then Sokrates delivers a rebuke, accusing him of trying to stir up trouble between himself and Agathon. So the traditional erotic triangle comes poking up through gentlemanly protocols and symposiastic gamesmanship: Alkibiades loves Sokrates who loves Agathon whose love is undeclared. Just then the party is invaded by a crowd of revellers. Chaos ensues. A great deal of wine is drunk. Many hours pass but by dawn most of the guests have gone home or passed out on the floor. Only Agathon, Aristophanes and Sokrates are still there, still awake, still drinking, still philosophizing. Around sunrise Agathon and Aristophanes doze off. Sokrates tucks them into their cloaks and goes his way.

do you like the films of Eric Rohmer
no
do you like the films of Eric Rohmer
sorry
do you like jam
it still leaves God untouched
do you like the films of Eric Rohmer
I find realistic techniques delightful
do you like jam
yes during the night
do you like the films of Eric Rohmer
don't know
do you like jam
it is in my thoughts a lot

do you neaten your bed in the morning
yes most almost always
do you neaten your bed in the morning
why
because of my baby bunny she'd lay little poops all over

SHORT TALK ON HOMER AND JOHN ASHBERY

Homer's *Odyssey* Book 24: the souls of the suitors all go down to Hades. Hermes leads them, all gibbering like bats, past the white rock of Leukas other underworld landmarks. Past the δῆμον ὀνείρων, which Homer leaves undescribed and unexplained. Δῆμος is "people, population or country." Ὄνειρος, "dream." A demographic of dreams. My friend Stanley Lombardo, translator, translates it "the dream deme." So how would this work? Big file catalogue with all the dreams waiting in alphabetical order to slip into some head at night? Or they're standing around with drinks? Or so bored by signifying they lie on the ground in heaps? Have a gift shop? Sell books by Adorno? Form factions and animosities? Perch on chairs like an audition? Smell of sweat? Exhaustion and tears? Or are they blissed beyond meaning, barefoot, organized by gentle bells? Do they practice all the time to keep in dream shape or is it more like perfect pitch? Are there dream trees to shade them, small dream boys who hide up there playing with fire while mothers search down below, losing heart? Do the dream streets fill with mobs sifting fast and slow at once over the sidewalk, each person sealed into a private membrane as clear and dense and general as death? If there are dogs in the dreams do they need to be walked? If Freud is there, is he aloof or enjoying himself? Down the road from the summer cottage of my friend Stanley Lombardo is a farm where emus and llamas graze. On the fence a sign informs us, "Llamas hum to their young." Do not worry, the sign implies, humming is okay. Does the demographic of dreams emit a worrying sound? Emus are in appearance plucky and plunging creatures, mostly torso. Llamas are stately, with an air of deep comedy, and larger than they seem. "You hit one of those you can say goodbye to your car," commented Stanley Lombardo, translator. He told me llamas never stop moving their ears even asleep. Whether they stop moving them asleep inside a dream is a question to be considered in a forthcoming *Short Talk on Stanley Lombardo*, where I hope to compare Stanley Lombardo with John Ashbery as a personality disposed to careless joy in any situation. A few years ago I attended an interview in which John Ashbery was present technologically due to being almost 90 years old and tired. The interviewers were a little afraid of him. Two interviewers. Groping for a way to engage a conversation. One mentioned a book she claimed John Ashbery had written entitled *Light*. Ashbery denied this. She insisted. She had the book at home on her bookshelf. Ultimately they decided it was an issue of *ARTnews* magazine on this theme. "So, John, can you say something about that?" asked the other interviewer, to which Ashbery after a long pause replied, "Light. What would we do without it?"

what is your philosophy of time
I feel like in a giant chestnut
what is your philosophy of time
I'm quite sure we'll surrender
what is your philosophy of time
how it's sweet and how it moves
what is your philosophy of time
it is a way to travel
what is your philosophy of time
a shallow closet with narrow bench and a rope to pull you up
what is your philosophy of time
thin cradle of feathers

POVERTY REMIX (Sestina)

1.

Poverty is a scapegoat.

We drive them out!

"Hermes, I shiver like crazy, give Hipponax a cloak."

(Don't look it in the eyes.)

We forbid you asking "in God's name" for bread.

We distinguish relative (some teeth) from absolute (no teeth) poverty by an
   algorhythm.

2.

Hipponax invented a poetic metre called "limping iambic," deliberately
   ugly in rhythm.

Longing and violence, built up over a lifetime? Unload it on the scapegoat!

Did you think the Black Death, with its depopulation of Europe by one-
   third, would bring an abundance of bread?

Instead everything ran out!

Stinginess blazed from all eyes.

Never mind morals, no one had a fig or a cloak.

3.

Beware the ruses and swindles of the poor, many of whom already *have* a
   cloak.

You say, Is poverty so different? We want things, it wants things, similar
   rhythm?

Note: shame lives upon the lids of the eyes.

First we wash you in the angels' tenderness, dear little filthy farting goat -
   then out!

(Well yes, *we* keep all the bread.)

4.

We forbid you using the God-card casually, for bread.

We forbid you touching our cloak.

No gloves, here's a dollar, no hands, out!

And this Hipponax, who was he, with his scatological girls and cock-shaker
rhythm?

Buffoon? Imposter? Caricaturist? Scapegoat?

Hunger came "parching" out of his eyes.

5.

We have a little game: take turns looking in the eyes

of that filthy farting one with his filthy farting bread who (we're sure) has
volunteered to go forth as scapegoat

from the folds of our sacred civic cloak and the beat of our reddish-foam
rhythm.

Count 4 when you breathe in and 6 when you breathe out!

6.

Tell me, is "drive them out" the same as "have stones for eyes"

sung in a shame-resistant extragrammatical grand-nasty mother-fig-fucker
flogged rhythm that soaks the bread

in blood and rips the cloak

off the scaped goat?

[*envoi*]

Why does poverty exist? Because stinginess does -

in its macroeconomic (law-of-demand-and-demand) cloak,

in its ritual-pharmakos (we-beat-them-with-branches) cloak,

in its they-might-be-faking-it (pity-and-barley cakes) cloak,

in its war-against-idleness (we're-all-debts-owed-to-death) cloak,

in its "enough-if-they-do-not-die-of-hunger-or-cold" (Martin Luther) cloak.

Give Hipponax a cloak.

Give Hipponax a cloak.

Give Hipponax a cloak.

Appendix 1: on pharmakos (φαρμακός)

Official name of one sacrificed as an atonement for others or to cleanse a community. Scapegoat. Necessary theater of a good community conscience. A word that quarrels with itself. *Pharmakos* is cognate with *pharmakon*, which means "poison" and "medicine," both at the same time, so logically a scapegoat is both saviour and source of the problem, both taint and cure. A presence (dirt) solved by its own absence. Hipponax describes the ritual: choose an animal or person (ugly, vagrant, criminal, deformed). Lead him out of wherever he is. Garland him. Beat him with fig branches seven times on the genitals. Drive him from the city. It was nice if the scapegoat offered itself voluntarily. Wine or milk might be poured on an animal's forehead, causing it to shake this off, taken as a gesture of assent. Or a person might be lured by luxuries - fed richly on special foods (barley cakes, cheese, black and white figs) for a day or a year before sacrifice.

Appendix 2: on shame (αἴδως)

Lonely people are ashamed of their solitude. Adults are ashamed of the children seeing. Rich people are ashamed of plastic bags. Poor people too. Not the same bags. Children are ashamed of the weirdest things and it haunts them through life. Aunt Shirley was ashamed of wearing pants to church. Was Wordsworth ashamed of taking poetic phrases from Dorothy's journals? Hard to know. Shame lives on the eyelids, according to an ancient Greek proverb. How you meet another's eyes, a question of status, of spiritedness, of the red dab on your hem. Sisters and brothers have a special shape of shame between them, like a dance notation no one else can read. Dorothy and William would at times lean together utterly helpless with laughing. At her kitchen door Dorothy welcomed vagrants (as they were then called) who regaled her with tales that she passed on to William.

Appendix 3: on Ploutos (Πλοῦτος)
One of the names the ancient Greeks gave to Death was Ploutos, which means Wealth. They celebrated him on tombstones with a sort of nihilist glee, as in the epitaph by Simonides of Keos that reads:

We are all debts owed to Death.

Ultimately Ploutos is the king of stingy: everyone gets added to his real estate and he never pays any of us back. We admire him. Envy him. But really, it's just a pile of dirt.

Appendix 4: on stinginess (οτενοχωρία)
Theophrastus divides stinginess into three aspects:
1 μικρλογία (*mikrologia*) "minute calculation of expense"
2 άνελευθερία (*aneleutheria*) "lack of freedom in giving"
3 αίσχροκεδεία (*aischrokerdeia*) "shameless grabbing at profit."

Sometimes I get used to seeing a certain homeless person on a certain street corner, then one day that person is gone. Giving rise to anxiety. And a measure of relief. I keep my dollar. Avoid shame. I am confused. Shame is confused. We are all stingy. Wordsworth was stingy. According to Emerson, who visited him in his cottage, Wordsworth offered guests one piece of bread and one cup of tea for dinner, if they wanted more they had to pay.

Appendix 5: on *miasma* (μίασμα)
As if walking between two fires I used to go north on 6th Avenue on my way to the YMCA pool, past homeless people on both sides of the street, some in blankets, some with a handwritten cardboard, some with a dog or dogs, some mad haters, some tending an inner world, some saying "God bless you" to all who pass, some very funny. I give a dollar or two dollars. Or bring all my quarters from home. Buy a homeless person a cup of coffee. Offer him a meal of barley cakes, cheese, black and white figs, then flog him on his genitals and drive him out of the city. Purification, says Plato, is part of

the science of division, "the kind of division that retains what is better and expels what is worse" (*Sophist*, 226d). I have many reasons for not wanting to be touched. For "touched" read tainted, polluted, defiled, dirtied, mixed up. Dirt is matter out of place. Who names the place? Remember the closet of Mr. Jaggers, the lawyer in Dickens' *Great Expectations*, where he "washed his clients off, as if he were a surgeon or a dentist . . ." Mr. Jaggers washes again after a dinner party. Who is pure?

Appendix 6: on Hipponax (Ἱππῶναξ)
Hipponax is a mystery (6th century BC). His style a challenge. His shamelessness an education. His poems treat of people who are poor, cold, hungry, angry, begging, criminal, deformed, iridescent with reasons to be unhappy. He talks about gulping and whipping and stooped-over women, about millet and filth-holes and his own soul. Describes drinking out of a pail because his cup broke. Gives literature its first instance of "motherfucker" (μητροκοίτης, fr. 12W). Calls someone who is starving "knife-in-the-belly" (fr. 32W). Knows a lot about hunger. Reported by Ovid to have died of hunger himself. Unlikely. But watch out. Angry ghost. Threat to the public good. He talks of scapegoats. He talks of shame. Later sources say he was ugly, deformed, fractious. That when mocked for his deformity he responded with songs so bitter his mockers killed themselves. Shame puts a pressure on poetic diction. Yet shame likes nothing more than to thrust shame aside. Shame is shameless. Shame has fun selling itself as an artistic *persona*. We don't know if Hipponax was really poor (the poor are tricky). But if it is true there was an ancient genre of poetry devoted to dramatizing the adventures and misadventures of the underclass, then we are thrown into turmoil about whom to give a dollar to, whom to whip on his genitals, whom to reprint in a bilingual edition.

Appendix 7: on being of two minds (διχόνοος)

Whether or not the scapegoat was ultimately killed is a question that fascinates and divides scholarly opinion. The evidence is all over the place. Callimachus (fr. 90) states unequivocally that the chosen one was merely chased over the border, possibly with stones, but not put to death. Tzetzes says that Hipponax says the scapegoat was fed fat, then garlanded, then beaten, then killed, then burned, then thrown in the sea. But Tzetzes lived centuries after Hipponax, who was anyway a poet and may have made stuff up. What is unmistakable in the sources, literary and historical, is the ambiguity people felt about dealing death to one of their own. My favourite story is from an ancient town called Leukas, where a victim sentenced to be thrown from a rock into the sea had birds and feathers fastened to him and a boat waiting below to take him over the border. Who is pure? Remember the librarian in the rare books room who made you put on white linen gloves before touching a book? Now the gloves are thought to be less clean than you are. Every touch is a modified blow, anthropologists say, but more to the point, every touch is dirt. Can you fall asleep if you haven't washed your face and cleaned your teeth? How did the scapegoat sleep, the night before the ritual, on his strip of cardboard over the subway grate, holding his garland out of the dust of the street with one hand, wondering whether to eat or save the pocketful of barley cakes for later?

Appendix 8: on rhythm (ῥυθμός)

It strikes me to wonder about the relation between motion and economic status. Middle-class people "go running." This would horrify Adorno, for whom even running for the bus had implications. "Running in the street conveys an impression of terror. . . . Once people ran from dangers too desperate to turn and face and someone running after a bus unwittingly bears witness to past terror. . . . Human dignity insisted on the right to walk, a rhythm not extorted by command or terror" (*Minima Moralia*, p. 162). I have seen rock stars run onto the stage but this is the *faux* terror of fame. Queens and kings and popes and governors move in a way that is called "stately," they carry the state on or with them, this is heavy. But what is the rhythm of poverty? Homeless people sit on the sidewalk, beggars stand fairly still. If a visibly poor or homeless person were running in the street he would be assumed to have stolen something and might be shot in the back by police. That poor soul who often stands on the corner outside my building, who is unusually tall and deeply mad, has a motionlessness that gathers itself around itself like a tree. Grand, regardless, like a tree. That tree might very well blow down in a storm but it will never just walk away.

do you like jam
yes
do you like the films of Eric Rohmer
don't know
do you like jam
not a fan
do you like the films of Eric Rohmer
I am curious now
do you like jam
very much
do you like the films of Eric Rohmer
sexy
do you like the films of Eric Rohmer
very much
do you like the films of Eric Rohmer
no idea
do you like jam
I do
do you like the films of Eric Rohmer
Love in the Afternoon is fantastic
do you like jam
yes when in need
do you like jam
do you like the films of Eric Rohmer
too sugary
do you like the films of Eric Rohmer
sorry
do you like the films of Eric Rohmer
no
do you like jam
it leaves God untouched
do you like the films of Eric Rohmer
I find realistic techniques delightful
do you like jam
yes during the night
do you like the films of Eric Rohmer
don't know
do you like jam
it is in my thoughts

SATURDAY NIGHT AS AN ADULT

We really want them to like us. We want it to go well. We overdress. They are narrow-boned people (art people), offhand, linens. It is early summer, first hot weekend. We meet on the street, jumble about with kisses and *Are we late?* They *had* been late, we'd half decided to leave, well. That place across the street, think we went there once, looks closed, says open, well. People coming out. Okay. Inside is dark, cool, oaken. Turns out they know the owner. He beams, ushers, we sit. And realize at once two things, first, the noise is unbearable, two, neither of us knows the other well enough to say, *Bag it*. Our hearts crumble. We order food by pointing and break into two yell factions, one each side of the table. He and she both look exhausted, from (I suppose) doing art all day and then the new baby. We eat intently as if eating were conversation. We keep passing the bread. My fish comes unboned, I weep. Pretend allergies. Finally someone pays the bill. We escape to the street. For some reason I was expecting snow outside. There is none. We decide not to go for ice cream and abruptly part, a little more broken. Saturday night as an adult, so this is it. We thought we'd be Nick & Nora, not their blurred friends in greatcoats. We cover our ears inside our souls. But you can't stop it that way.

what is your philosophy of time
I hear Heraklitos whisper in the waves

what is your philosophy of time
just smile
what is your philosophy of time
pills can help
what is your philosophy of time
yes during the night
what is your philosophy of time
nasty
what is your philosophy of time
sorry
what is your philosophy of time
no mirrors
what is your philosophy of time
what is your philosophy of time
what is your philosophy of time
what is your philosophy of time
what is your philosophy of time
what is your philosophy of time
what is your philosophy of time
what is your philosophy of time
what is your philosophy of time
what is your philosophy of time
what is your philosophy of time
what is your philosophy of time
what is your philosophy of time
what is your philosophy of time
what is your philosophy of time
what is your philosophy of time

SNOW

One cold dark night there was a story about a knocking at the outer gate. Despite cries of Yes! Yes! Coming! someone still knocked and the snow that had piled on the gate was blown halfway up the door itself, with no meaning as to the blind knocking or the thick snow or why it did not stop. I knew I should be writing a straightforward story, or even a poem, but I didn't. I should get back to words, I thought, plain words.

I had been looking at the New Testament in the side-by-side (Greek and Latin) version edited by Johannes Leusden in 1801, which I'd found on my bookshelf in a fragile state that did not allow the pages to be turned quickly. Little flecks broke off. I opened it at random to First Corinthians 10, a letter of Paul's about idolatry. The letter spoke of people who wandered in the wilderness eating "pneumatic" bread and drinking from a "pneumatic" rock, or so I was translating it in my head, the word for "spiritual" being *pneumatikos* in Greek, from *pneuma*, "breath." Can either bread or rock be made of breath? Anyway who can drink from a rock? A sort of dreariness, like a heavy smell of coats, comes down on the word "spiritual" and makes religion impossible for me. The page is turned. Flecks fall.

Before turning the page though, I noticed that Paul's text, in the verse following the pneumatic rock, was at pains to identify the rock with Christ (that is, God) and to explain that the rock was "following" these people through the desert so they could drink from it. How very awkward, I thought. I wondered why God couldn't come up with a better water arrangement for these people and why Paul couldn't find a more graceful image of God's care. Presumably Paul wants people to seek and cherish God's care? But to visualize the longed-for Other bumping along behind your desert caravan in the form of a rock might just make you morose or confused.

Confused and morose myself, not least of all because of that continued knocking at the gate, and in need of a fresh idea, I opened the Bible again and found Psalm 119. This seemed to be another text about people in the wilderness:

81 My soul fainteth for thy salvation: but I hope in thy word.

82 Mine eyes fail for thy word, saying, When wilt thou comfort me?

83 For I am become like a bottle in the smoke; yet do I not forget thy statutes.

And all at once I recognized it as a passage I had worked on before, at a time when snow was not my concern - I'd been invited to give a lecture on (as I recall) "the idea of the university," a topic about which I knew very little, and so began to compose a lecture more concerned with the word "Idea" than the concept "university." I'm not clear on whether I ever delivered this lecture: I can't find it among my papers. Three days before the lecture date my mother died. I fell to my knees in the kitchen. Astoundedness was like a silvery-white fog that seeped up and over all those days. I had visited her only a week before, the long train, then bus, then taxi trip. She seemed okay. Forbidden by her doctor from her nightly glass of Armagnac she'd taken to dabbing it behind her ears. The word "idea" comes from ancient Greek, "to see." Was there a way to get out of giving that lecture, I wondered.

Psalm 119.83 is an outcry: "For I am become like a bottle in the smoke; yet do I not forget thy statutes," in the King James version. In more modern versions, "For I am like a wineskin shrivelled by smoke"; or "Though I am shrivelled like a leather flask in the smoke"; or "I am useless as a discarded wineskin." The notion seems to be that without God the psalmist or his life becomes dry, sooty, wrinkled and worn, dark and dismal, parched, disfigured, miserable, bereft of spiritual moisture. There is a strand of tradition that reads "hoarfrost" in place of "smoke" but no one knows what to do with that. The same week my mother died my boyfriend left. (Beware the conversation that begins, "Do you think people should be completely honest with one another?") We'd been together a number of years but he was young and closeness to death made him queasy. Do I blame him? I admit I was not a very erotic person at the time. And well, my quotient of astoundedness was full. He drove me to the funeral and more or less kept going. I more or less waved goodbye.

There was no question I had to get out of giving that lecture.

The odd thing is, I can't remember if I did or did not (get out of the lecture). The chronology is a blur. I do remember sitting in an armchair, at the very brink of an armchair, hands fisted in my lap, facing the Professor of Religious Studies who had commissioned the lecture. I was pleading for a cancellation or deferral. He sat tightly contained on the far side of his big desk. He was pale. Alarmed. He may have been a priest. Tears poured down my face. I told him of my mother's outlandish little red car coat. He was not a chaotic person. A large feeling of cul-de-sac filled the room. Beyond that I can recover only a few mental screenshots of me speaking about bottles and smoke to a dusty lecture hall of people with crossed legs, but these may be shards of some anxiety dream, not a credible memory.

Historically the first instance of the noun *idea* in ancient Greek is in an epinician ode of Pindar (*Pythian* 10.103) praising an Olympic victor "beautiful with respect to his idea," that is, his appearance. Plato's use of the word to designate things like "the form of the good" is familiar. Slightly stranger perhaps, Demokritos' choice of *atomoi ideai* (literally "uncut shapes") to mean the indivisible elements of his atomic theory. Best of all is Matthew's phrasing in the final chapter of his Gospel to describe the look of the angel who came down from heaven, rolled back the door of Christ's tomb and sat on it (28.3):

ἥ ἰδέα αὐτοῦ ἦν ὡς ἀστραπή
The idea of him was like lightning.

"And his garment shone white as snow," continues Matthew's Gospel, reminding me to go to the door and see who was knocking - has it stopped? - but there is a sense of suspension in the night air, as of a person not quite turning away to go back on their own footprints through the deepening snow. Snow can deepen fast on nights like this. The reason I went to visit my mother, the week before her death, was a dream I had. A young man in red epaulets was ministering to a room of restless guests who lay fully clothed in bathtubs. Waking suddenly (3 a.m.) I knew the young man in red epaulets as the night clerk in the hotel where I stayed when I visited her. Strange choice for a psychopomp, I thought, as hours later the train glided west in a weak tarnish of dawn. There was ground fog everywhere, then afternoon sunlight (the bus) so deep you could enter it as a lake. Finally a taxi gliding past people in their kitchens.

The weekend was spent watching her sleep, oxygen shunting on and off. When awake she glared wildly, or ate small dabs of ice cream, or, once, spent a few minutes studying a photograph I'd brought her (of myself at a posh artists' retreat on Lake Como) then said, Why did you wear your glasses? I was not with her when she died. I assume the young man in red epaulets showed up and that he let her wear her car coat. She loved that red car coat.

Last thing: one Sunday evening about a year before all this we were on the telephone, my mother and I; it was just after we sold the house and she'd moved to the facility, where she was allowed a small sensible room and a few possessions. As we talked I was watching snow drift down the dusk outside, counting it, one hundred and five, one hundred and six, one hundred and seven, when out of a pause she said, "It's funny to have no home" - funny being a funny word for what she meant. I say this now to remind myself how words can squirt sideways, mute and mad; you think they are tools, or toys, or tame, and all at once they burn all your clothes off and you're standing there singed and ridiculous in the glare of the lightning. I hung up the phone. I stared at the snow for some time. I expect she did too.

do you neaten your bed in the morning
yes
why
small ceremonies are good for the soul
do you neaten your bed in the morning
yes
why
once I slept in a contrabass case maybe I told you
do you neaten your bed in the morning
no
why
I live alone
do you neaten your bed in the morning
sometimes
why

THE VISITORS

visitor (noun) caller, guest, transient, visitant, habitué (French), passenger, newcomer, latecomer, Johnny-come-lately (see ARRIVAL)

Friday morning

What are these people doing here? I wake up and the house is full of them. Did I invite them? I don't think so. I listen at my door. How to avoid bumping into visitors on my way to the bathroom. My bathroom is somewhat hidden, maybe they won't find it. Maybe they won't find any bathroom and will go home. I look up "visitor" in *Roget's Thesaurus*, a handy reference tool I keep in my room.

Reading *Roget's* has its usual calming effect. Words - oh I don't know - dangling their little roots in the past as they reach forward, reach towards us. And *Roget's* tidy pages, the beautiful lists, all those analogical children of slight difference - it is the opposite of anarchy! No maybe not. I suppose you know why Roget made lists. Chronic mental instability in several members of his family including himself led him to seek what Freud might call a *coping mechanism*. Roget made lists of lots of things, not just words. Posterity has not found much use for his tallies of "things in the garden" or "the movements of the iris of the eye." But his *Thesaurus* enjoyed 28 reprintings in his lifetime. He lived to be 90 and dabbled in a variety of scientific researches, e.g., "Explanation of an optical deception in the appearance of the spokes of a wheel seen through vertical apertures," a paper he presented to the Royal Society of London in 1824, thus more or less inventing the movies. Freud would have liked Roget.

Friday afternoon

Are they religious? Is this some kind of ritual weekend? I am no longer calm. I glimpsed a woman in white on the stairs. I heard someone rummaging in the kitchen. I descend to confront - a visitor! After the jam? Yes I think so. Or the gin. I don't care about the gin. I am keeping the jam for the fox. No! he says, we're making a movie! We'll use seven rooms of the house plus the porch! All at once! Rehearse today, shoot tomorrow! Single take! He is very excited. He talks in exclamation marks like Don Quixote. I ask what the movie's about. Sex divorce fighting longing realness pretending! he says. Not jam? I say and we both laugh. His is a guilty laugh.

Roget had no fox, no fox pocket. Even as a child he couldn't relax, he was compulsively neat. His first word list, compiled at age 8, would continue to be perfected till his death in 1869. He organized the first edition of the *Thesaurus* (1852) in 1,002 concepts. When Roget stared into the fire he was thinking out a problem. Next day by reclassifying "absence of intellect" as a subcategory of "intellect" and "indiscrimination" as a subcategory of "choice," he pared *Roget's* down to a neat 1,000. Would Freud have liked me? I don't think so. His favoured patients tended to be arty types, girls but not girlish - Hilda Doolittle, for example, who describes her experience of analysis with Freud as the most luscious sort of *vers libre*. Sometimes when they were talking H.D. and Freud let the telephone ring on and on. We trapped each other, she says, but his wings held. What does that mean? *His wings held.* I'd like to draw Freud with his fox. I'm not good at wings. When not drawing I am incongruous (inappropriate, inapt, improper, incompatible, irreconcilable, inconsistent, unusual, warring, strange, alien).

Saturday morning

My bathroom! As predicted! I stumble in, door not locked, there lies a visitor in the tub *in flagrante*, guitar on his lap, head flung back to the wall, mouth agape with song, huge naked white foot propped on the taps. This foot projects towards me. This foot is a beachcomber, a beachhead, a beacon, a beast, a bedlam, words fail me. It resembles the dead Christ's foot in Mantegna's *Lamentation of Christ*, but we know from art history that Mantegna had to scale down the size of Christ's foot lest it block our view of Christ's violently foreshortened legs, torso and face. No scale-down with this visitor - splayed out in the bath in his headphones he laughs, he twangs, he flashes his blue eye-guns at me and cries, I love the tension!

Faced with Christ's unforeshortened foot, I retreat to the stairs. What a maelstrom in me. Headphones in the bath! Well, I can't worry about that. Let me just say, these visitors are no Éric Rohmer. They claim to be making a movie. Spent yesterday in seven different rooms of the house, not to mention the bathroom, playing and singing louder and louder until by evening the whole place was wailing like a dinosaur. Rohmer wore earplugs while shooting the nightclub scenes of *Full Moon in Paris*, a fine romantic comedy of his that (most people don't notice) has a fox in the corner of one scene. "Éric Rohmer" of course is a pseudonym - his real name being Maurice [something] - his mother never knew he made films, she thought he was a high school teacher all his life. Watch for the fox.

To enter the door of the drawing is uncanny.

More on Roget. One morning in 1820 he was gazing out the basement window of his house. Saw a man with horse and cart passing and noticed (vertical blinds) how the spokes of the cart's moving wheels appeared to be curved. He dashed up to the street. Paid the man to drive back and forth several times. Made mathematical calculations. The human retina, he had discovered, typically saw a fast series of still images as a continuous movie. The fox opens and closes in my pocket. Tomorrow the fox will look for the door to enter my drawing.

Did I mention my admiration for Éric Rohmer, yes I think so. In adolescence I used to watch his movies with pencil and paper in hand, alert for quotes to use with older women. *Oh how he shattered the spirit world, as Pascal said of Archimedes*, is a good one. Also I loved the way Jean-Louis Trintignant pronounced *boy scoot* and his awful haircut. Why am I telling you this? Because Éric Rohmer knew how to make a movie. Keep everybody in the same room, is a good first rule. And who is this woman wandering the halls in white satin undergarments? Do they know her? They demur. Her whiteness makes me dream. She is always going out of rooms just as I come in - it's like living in the New Wave: *I am a bachelor, I am mysterious.*

Saturday afternoon

Sneaking about the halls, eavesdropping here and there, I learn a few things. They are from Iceland, these visitors, which explains a lot. Perhaps you've been to Iceland? I went once, I couldn't stay. There is nothing there but emptiness. A gigantic empty wind wails along the edge of every minute and tosses the odd dazed seabird out onto the empty beach. When you drive the single lonely highway, a huge piece of emptiness drives along beside you and goes wherever you go, then piles up in your driveway at home on top of the emptinesses from other days. You see horses standing in the fields so soaked with emptiness they can't move, they've been there for years, they might as well be waterfalls. Of course all this exerts a psychic pressure on inhabitants - the whole soul frays. I made lists while I was there. I took photographs too, but later at home found the emptiness had vanished from each one, leaving a tiny print. Pawprint, handprint, mouthprint, I can't tell.

The most uncanny thing about my fox is whether or not he will find the door.

Saturday night

I ask one of the visitors for his theory of mimesis. My heart is a yacht! he cries, quoting some 9th-century saga, no doubt. Then he tells me a long story about his godmother whose name was Engel and who (he claims) knew Freud. In fact Freud invited Engel to his house in London to play the piano. Back in Berlin she had been a popular performer of *Lieder* in sparse modernist arrangements and had been invited by Hitler to do a private concert. *Nein*, said Engel and left for London on the next train. But it turned out Freud had no piano in his London house, only a clavichord. The punch line to this story involves the words "Klavier" and "Komplex" in a bit of

Germanic wordplay that the visitor finds so hilarious he loses his balance in the kitchen and knocks over a row of jam jars. There will be a lot of tidying up to do after they leave. Engel made a Freud joke with Freud! he exclaims. The fox is chewing off old bits of the fur behind his leg. His leg is beginning to look like Jean-Louis Trintignant.

But his wings held. I keep returning to this occluded comment. I sense a treacherous nature. And there she goes again, the woman in white satin undergarments, what is she up to? Is she wounded? Is she Engel? Is she one of the Ten Commandments? Or is she asleep, a dream residue, one of those agile vegetative processes whose activity (Freud says) is doubled as we drift off? A better question might be, why is Freud's jargon so catchy? Vernacular, dialect, cant, argot, idiom, lingo, patois, patter, slang, jive (slang), gobbledygook (colloquial), technology. Are children terrifying? Yes I think so - they undress, they catch fire, they go to paradise. But they have no power. Freud knew, the fox has the power.

Sunday

My fox gets trembly when there are farewells. I'm not sure if he is sad or glad or just wants jam. Hilda Doolittle's final image of her analytic time with Freud: him beating his fist on the sofa, saying, I am an old man, you do not think it worth your while to love me! Eros, amor, infatuation, crush, flame, passion, desire, attraction, venery, tender feelings, yearning, devotion, fancy, attachment, adoration, idolatry, worship, wooing, serenading, romance, intrigue, tryst. So as the day darkens toward evening I resume my perch on the stairs and monitor goings-on below. I see all the visitors' souls one by one slide back into their bodies and scamper off down a grassy slope to the river. I should return to my drawing but feel a need to check the house for traces and, so to speak, piss on all the boundaries. Freud in his heyday would have called this a homosexually-tinged desire. Freud was prim. In old age he looked like a shrunken monkey, according to Engel, and when she visited him to play his clavichord, he whispered in her ear, *I was infamous not famous.* Poor rosy-cheeks, what did he really want? Now the halls of the house stand empty. Faint ticking or dripping sounds. Have the microphones been left on?

Yes, think so. A tech guy appears, switching off lights. He goes from room to room. I sit in the dark, I am patient. Later we will try the drawing again. The fox breathes with the night, with the stars. In and out he breathes.

do you neaten your bed in the morning and why
how do you sustain morale during a long project
do you like jam
do you use anyone else's toothpaste, skin products or pills when these are left in the

THRET

Part I: WE POINT THE BONE

Little tough ones, little tall ones, like little tall trees, others yellow as hay, their tiny blades falling across the cracks, the stones. Blades moving a bit. There is no reason for you to wonder about this. Keep listening. Keep glancing out, small grasses in the driveway, perhaps following two lines of thought at once as a person does on the telephone on an ordinary day, little grasses like that pushing up, thrusting their way, can be expected in time to dissect and over-turn the whole driveway and how strange this voice you do not recognize is using your name, talking about you as *he*, saying he had an accident, very bad accident. Very bad, taken to the hospital. Very bad, hospital, must proceed at once. He? You? No staircases go up to this moment where you perceive the second person cut from the third person within you and it all drops off into a past tense that will not have happened yet. Click. Dial tone. The little grasses look weak and cold. Pity them. Don't pity them. Watch yourself. You didn't know the blades hung in your mouth.

The word "threat" comes from Old English *thret*, coercion, and Middle High German *dröz*, annoyance, also associated with the Latin verb *trudere*, to push, thrust, shove. People so pushed will leave town for a while, six months, a year, return quietly. See how things go. Resume as they say normal life. Keep listening, keep an ear cocked. Wake up stinging. You will dream of a man who hastens along pulling off a piece of his face as he goes, drops it on the sidewalk. Telephones are not the only way. You receive your own obituary in the mail. A person in black stops before you in the street then hurries away. And suddenly, at six in the morning, as if swept by winter rivers, everything changes. Your telephone, your kitchen, your driveway, all these things that had a notion of you now change their gaze and watch you from a different place - no, two places. Everything now happens from two places. You brush your teeth in the second and in the third person. You stand at the window in the second and in the third person, watching the driveway, waiting perhaps for your child who is late from school. You sweat from those places.

So I was crossing the schoolyard one morning. Saturdays I go to early bike class at the gym and often take a shortcut through the yard behind the local schoolhouse where there are swings and monkey bars and a sort of roughly paved basketball court with benches for parents. I love the clear empty light of Saturday morning. There's no one in the schoolyard at that hour except usually a guy reading a newspaper.

He sits not on the benches but on the edge of a low stone retaining wall that marks off the paved area from the swings. He balances exactly on the wall with one leg crossed over the other and doesn't look up. It's funny you can tell just from how a person sits reading the newspaper that he is, as they say, off the grid in some essential way. Economically. Mentally. Who knows. I don't like to say homeless. He's not unclean. He wears regular clothes, a sort of sports coat, he has no collection of stuff parked nearby, just his newspaper. Yet he is different, sharper, sharpened on the air. He and I don't look at one another straight. I cross the schoolyard briskly, normally. He is on my left as I cross. I do not feel his eyes on my back when I exit via the little path that runs along the sixth-grade science classroom, past the two old steelcase doors still marked *Boys* and *Girls*, onto the street.

But that one morning when I crossed the yard he wasn't there. I registered this with half my mind, I was a bit late and had put my T-shirt on backwards, the label was bothering my neck, anyway I kept going, stepped onto the little path, glanced into the dark science classroom, smoothed down my hair and was almost to the street when something white that had been pushing itself up through my attention on the left formed into a thought. White thing. Boys. Girls. I stopped and turned.

In the place where he would have been sitting on the wall was a whiteness like a pile of paper. I don't have time to investigate this, I thought, I'm already late, and I turned onto the street. A crease went through me, that's the way it felt, a piece of me folded over in a crease inside and lay flat, knife-edged. I stopped, turned again, went back. The white pile looked like pieces of torn newspaper, words torn out, heaped on the stone wall. No not words, single letters. Careful job of tearing. I was late for my class but I had to stop and sit down on the wall and study them, arranging the letters this way and that. Nine letters. Alphabetically: ABDELLMOO. Other ways: DOLOMBEAL, MOBELLADO, BADLELOOM, BLOODMEAL. *Bloodmeal.* I paused. Looked at the red stain revealed by my moving the letters from where they'd been piled on the stone. A dark red stain. Recent but dry. I thought about the bike class, gave up on it. Glanced up the street and down the street. Quiet backyards in every direction, one behind the other, how deeply they nested like bowls of graded sizes, some empty, some cluttered, with their yew trees, their dropped toys, their clotheslines, their shadow. I am someone who knows about stains, it's my business. I do cleaning. Also I have occasionally been engaged as an expert witness in criminal investigations. Expert witnessing is well paid. Much can be inferred from a stain.

This one for example. I glanced up the street again, vaguely expecting to see the egret, then remembered it had been kidnapped. Some rich people (a judge and his striking Northern wife) who live up the street have an ornamental pond and used to keep a pet egret in the backyard until the judge fell afoul of certain local cocaine financiers and the egret got snatched. Ransom was paid. They slaughtered the egret anyway. Life went on for the judge who persevered in his efforts to clear our small town of drug trade. One day the local paper published a political cartoon about the judge, his involvement in some municipal controversy I can't remember now, and there in the background stood the tall white-skinned wife, balanced on one leg in what looked like an ornamental pond.

The judicial procedure was soon discontinued, technical reasons, and there went my hopes for a Xmas vacation in Rio. I'd been scheduled to testify about various stains found in various places at various crime scenes and, as I say, the pay is good.

But now back to BLOODMEAL. BLOODMEAL was furnishing me with several points to consider. Letters cut out with scissors, not sloppily done. Different fonts but all caps and roughly the same font size so the word, laid out on the retaining wall, looked emphatic but amiable, not crazy. The blood, for it was blood, showed a stain pattern not created by passive drops (gravity) but swiped onto the stone (human purpose), its viscosity indicating leakage from a lower extremity, not a major organ and not copious. It was a few hours old.

The body goes dark, inside and out, at times. The mind stops down to a narrowness. Why were they threatening me with minor wounds to a person I scarcely knew and didn't care about? This is meager, I thought, this is feeble, what a pallid degree of enemy I am to them! I was on some level insulted. Yet my reactions felt rudderless, I struggled to get hold of them. Let's review the facts, my facts. Mother and father gone. No children, wife or waterfowl. You'd have to grasp at straws to find a way of menacing me. I went to a conference of hemotophonomists in Krakow last year. People who analyze bloodstains for forensic purpose are a varied lot, as you might imagine, but a kind of bluff stoicism seems characteristic of them. Queasiness not an option. Pity not an option. Facts are what matter. Striding about the old stone streets of Krakow in the small hours of the night, I was listening to PJ Harvey on my headset and pondering ethical types. Every bloodspatter analysis is proof that strength alone cannot earn you the world, you with your bludgeon raised. *I can know you.* I can read your trace. People who do violence or who threaten to do violence do thereby to some extent reveal themselves. And I admit, rising from the retaining wall and stuffing BLOODMEAL into my pocket, I began almost to enjoy myself. Matching wits. It's the best thing in life. Clearly I would have to rethink my role in the war on drugs, at least locally, meanwhile I was involved with worthy opponents, intelligent maybe not but they understood close observation of facts. And their interest in the nuances of me would eventually show me their own. I felt cocky. I felt singular. I rose to my full outline, sharp and white against the day. *We point the bone.*

No more bike classes. I opened my research. Got all the old police reports, began sifting the judge's data, working out a certain picture of how things went down. During this time I stopped answering my cell phone and forgot to eat. There were a couple dozen packets of gummi bears in the fridge and some Ryvita, I subsisted on these. Also during this time occurred the action at the schoolhouse. I had to lean my head on my notebook and weep. Our local schoolmaster, a brave and innovative soul, decided to not pay the spring semester's installment of protection money and see where that led. It led to a Wednesday in March when the entire student body, give or take a few kids home with colds or flu, was mowed down by machine gun fire as it emerged for recess. Those chubby advancing knees. Boys. Girls. I wasn't enjoying myself anymore. Several nights I went and stood outside the judge's house, watched dark shapes move behind his blinds. The pond lay still.

Threat is a communication system that functions best with a high level of noise. My research had narrowed down to five people. I found out a lot about them, facts, every fact available. I used regular mail, priority mail, parcels, faxes, FedEx, a dead fox, money and messengers in black. I used sulfur, pollen, beet juice, blackberries, meat, ashes, urine, rust, semen, feces and blood of every type in my lab. I threatened everything those five people were or did or knew or hoped or had kinship with. I polluted every surface they met, touched or saw in the course of the day and every place their dreams went in the black sleep of night. I confused their categories and contaminated their information. One of them received a pizza with his wife's email password in black olives across the top (his mistress's, underneath, in roasted pepper). Next day both women changed their passwords. I sent another pizza. Does it sound like I was having a merry and mischievous time? In fact there was no mood I can name. Expert witness or not, it was all so clumsy, it was all so inadequate, so DIY. Nothing I did matched what they had done or tied off the loose ends of sin. I was flailing at trauma. I worked without realistic expectation of follow-through, I'm not much good at actual harm. Still, it felt better to me to live this way than to be circling my perfect calves on a bike at the gym. I meant to lower the quality of those five lives, just a bit, every minute of their lives that I could reach. Make a small mark, nothing sublime. You know that drop of the heart you feel when you turn and see *stain* on your best shirt. I lasted a couple of months.

In ancient times there were tribes who rode into battle shooting volleys of curses before them. Little papers attached to arrows such as those now fluttering down across my windows in a white storm, I do not see the wording. Feeling my way upstairs in the dark, some day I can't remember morning in, old mothy smell in my nose, how I hate carpeted stairs! why have I never replaced these stairs - I imagine the old tried-and-true language. May you walk wrong. May you never sleep again. May the cat eat you and the devil eat the cat. Go astray a hundred times. We point the bone. They will arrive this evening or possibly tomorrow. If I call don't pick up the phone. Let me leave a posthumous message. I've always wanted to do that.

THRET

Part II: ASPIRIN FOR TRAVELLERS

They did not kill me after all in the kill house. I'm still here. Still working stains and blood. Still listening to PJ Harvey. I've started going to bike class again. Not every Saturday but often. I take the shortcut. There's a guy on the wall again. Not the same guy. Sitting. He sits at an angle, uncomfortably, on the wall, gazing sort of down and off, with the constraint of an animal feeling itself watched. Meanwhile I go on with my sociopolitical action program. I have added an assistant to the program. His name is Short Pants. He befriended me during long afternoons at the kill house.

The qualities that endear Short Pants to me are alacrity and wrath. He also eats my garbage. Short Pants is a carrion crow. I saw him on a tree in the backyard. He saw me in the kitchen. I was eating toast. He seemed to know about toast. I opened the screen door and laid toast on the railing. He moved his eye onto it. We paused. That's for you, I said. That's for me, he said right back. It shouldn't have surprised me that he could talk. He has four pairs of labia embedded in the muscles of his throat and an auditory midbrain nucleus proportional in size to my own. But the grammar was surprising. How did he learn pronoun function? His voice had cracks in it. Suddenly he hurtled from the tree and toast was gone.

Short Pants and I share a narrow but nourishing social bond, also a politics. You recall I was harassing local drug lords previously. Short Pants and I persist in this.

The corvid brain thrives on a diet rich in protein and fat. Compared to other creatures' a crow's brain is big, can weigh up to 2.7% of body mass (cf. human brains at 1.9%) and more brain means more thinking. What is thinking. We call it thinking when data coming in from the world passes through and out of the brain *different than when it arrived*. I began laying out toast with peanut butter on the railing. Short Pants and I evolved our thinking on several topics gradually. I wouldn't exactly say I trained him, any more than he trained me. We each had a blank in us that got filled in.

Our first action involved the judge with the ornamental pond and the Northern wife. Since selling out to local criminal interests the judge had acquired new anxieties and a guard dog out back. I don't know much about dogs. Big black-and-tan fellow and what a barker. You could hear that dog all over town. Short Pants and I staked out the property a few days to get the pattern. Generally the dog slept till 7 or 7.30 a.m. when the judge came out in his Nikes, whistled three times and called the dog's name. The dog would explode from his sleep place and off they go down the street to the path by the lake. Short Pants had no trouble mastering the whistle and call. His talents go beyond mere mimicry - a firefly after all can mimic another firefly by some mindless reflexive *chingchingching* of cranial circuitry but to impersonate a ninth-circuit court judge so competently that his own dog can be induced to wake him with ecstatic cries at 4 a.m. nine days in a row required not only conscious and complex manipulation of all the musculature of Short Pants' throat but a philosophical awareness of the aims of human speech. Weekdays I waited in the schoolyard till I heard the barking then went home to lay out toast on the railing. Nine days of this and then the weather turned. Rain of an extreme nature was predicted and hurricane-force winds.

No doubt the autumn rains depress me. So, I'm sitting on the backporch watching the trees sway at the top and pondering the value of our activist efforts when Short Pants comes rattling out of the gloom and drops a gift on my knee. Two long thin strips of rubber. Facings from the windshield wipers on someone's vehicle, likely the big silver Maybach we'd seen parked in the judge's driveway most mornings. Short Pants had a good sense of *coda*.

Moving on. No one in our town drives a Maybach except it's been awarded to him by a certain person. You can't buy them anymore, not many of us were in the market anyway, but a certain person appears to have his own supply. This person's name is Tiplady and "*boasting lavish shit*" is how he puts it on his website under Tiplady's Harmless Pleasures. You might not think someone so deeply involved in the other kind of pleasures would be this frank on his website or even have a website but then Tiplady proves an exception to most rules of classical mechanics, common sense and social gesture. That he is dashingly and majestically generous to his friends, to waiters, to dancers in strip clubs, to the boys who detail his cars and the girls who buff his nails, seems an aspect of boasting. But can someone tell me *what is it* about Louis Vuitton? Why do gangsters love this stuff? It's just luggage, right? Whenever he's bored at home Tiplady drives out to the mall with a carload of people and drops in at the LV outlet. He consults every new item of stock, analyzes trends with the head salesman and never leaves without buying satchels or cartridge belts or monogrammed this and that for everybody who came along. A lot of people come along.

I'm not against altruism as such. I just wish Tiplady's unselfish impulses extended to the middle school children who buy ready rock from his runners at lunch hour behind the schoolhouse. It's an old lament but the fact is you can enslave a child's life so easily and Tiplady knows this, he knows education. He knows the price he gets for a rock from a 12-year-old barely covers the baking soda that went into it but a little addict is a bound-down future for the merchandise, a reliable crop. Tiplady gardens as he pleases.

Facts and accuracy are what I'm good at, speculation not so much. A blood-stained stocking for example. I never was one for standard puzzle-solving, crosswords, brainteasers. Stains and evidence, tracing the pattern, that's my expertise. The science of stains sort of runs a puzzle backwards. You're given the errors and chaos of how the answer went wrong, you work back to a right answer and maybe the original question. Recently I attended an auction of "Bonnie and Clyde Death Car Items" recovered from the floor of their bullet-pocked car on May 23, 1934, Arcadia, Louisiana, including:

silk stocking stained with blood
unspent .45 caliber bullet
single armature from a pair of eyeglasses one small wooden flathead screwdriver one small Bayer aspirin tin

Ambush is a shabby tactic but you get a sudden snapshot. They had been living in their car, where Bonnie wrote bad poetry and Clyde cared for his guns - or maybe not since the rifle jammed when he raised it to shoot on May 23. The aspirin tin is provocative. Aspirin for travellers. The tin is very small. It is empty. Who had a headache? And why did she take off one stocking? However I digress. What I started to say is that facts themselves no longer satisfy me. I am restless at a different level of accuracy. As far as facts go, I know who Tiplady is and what he is doing to our town. Crime, method of crime, perpetrator of crime, not a mystery. Something else hangs in my dream. A flock of crows, a horde, a hover, a misery, a muster, a murder, a parcel, a storytelling of crows, in their shapeless black overcoats, gathering, perhaps to mourn. Making that sound that crows make. Actually crows make two sounds. The *caaaaw* sound signals danger. The *haaaaw* refers only to meat.

Now that I'm old I wake up early. I like the sound of my shoes on empty streets at 5 a.m. The solidity of heels, the *klopklop* of a good horse on its way and I like my reasoning at that hour. Thoughts fall into slots, actions plan themselves. So it was while perambulating the streets of central downtown one morning at first light that I attained two clear realizations simultaneously:

1 the girlfriend
2 the oven

Not my girlfriend, not my oven. I had turned the corner of Front St. onto Esperanza and saw two black shapes frolicking in the airshaft between a tall bank and a high-rise. One unmistakably Short Pants, the other conjecturally his mate. They were riding the airshaft to the top of the bank, alternating with each other, hurling themselves headfirst into the updraft and snapping their wings open fast to catch the wind. On top they perched and exchanged remarks before plunging to the bottom to start over. The monogamy of crows is well known. I expected to see Fury (for that was her name) showing up on my backporch for peanut butter toast and I was not mistaken. But I get ahead of my story.

The vision of those two corvid playmates combining so simply and joyously with wild air made me halt and think. Two can be better than one. Could we apply this logic to Tiplady and if so how? My next action became clear then. Tiplady has a rival who operates from the outlet mall on the edge of town and who had to be discouraged from freelancing in Tiplady's territory a few years back. Discouragement took the form of popping three of the rival guy's street-level pitchers and a bit of mutilation thrown in to make it look Mexican. The rival guy backed off. The rival guy has a reputation for barging in and backing off as well as a general slipperiness, why they call him Swimsaway. But Swimsaway never swims entirely away and I'd heard rumours he was buying up weapons. Planning something. What if Tiplady and Swimsaway could be encouraged to think of one another as playmates again? What if they got the notion to harass, threaten, distract, detoxify or destroy one another, leaving our town temporarily or even permanently better off, the self-cleaning oven scenario?

It was a bonus as soon as Short Pants and I went into action that Fury joined in, proving herself a fast learner and decisive coactivist, with some sense of humour. Our program was one of continual minor delinquencies performed, usually at early dawn when corvid eyesight is most acute, upon Tiplady's premises, usage and pride. To confiscate his garbage-can lids, the windshield-wiper blades from his fleet of Maybachs, the votive candles from the shrine in his backyard and half the tail feathers of his pet peacock - but only from one side of the tail and only one feather at a time over many days so the bird grew gradually more unbalanced and at last toppled sideways on the grass - these were tasks that pleased all three of our childlike souls equally. White-washing the porch with excrement was not my idea, I just don't like mess, notwithstanding an image that I still cherish of the morning Fury managed to target Tiplady's bodyguard just as he emerged from the house in all his bulletproof puffery. However - if I may slightly boast, for the score was mine although the orchestration belonged entirely to the crows - our most elegant and efficacious action that season, doom aside, was the cigar switch. Some crows are very good at undoing packaging. Fury specialized in FedEx.

Now Tiplady was a vegan and a hypochondriac and had a box of homeo-pathic remedies delivered once a week (FedEx). The box remained on the porch until the bodyguard took it in but with the bodyguard now grown wary of porch appearances, the box might sit out for some time. Meanwhile I had rekindled my acquaintance with Swimsaway, whom I knew from court cases in the old days. Arraigned a few times, always got off. Something likable in him, less caught up in himself than other gangsters, one eye on the future, which he realistically expected to be bad. One eye too many as somebody said about Oedipus but my advice would be, don't start sympathizing with Swimsaway, don't go down that road. Lots of skeletons lined up on that road, lots of master-slave stuff, they all get into it these kingpins, stories abound. Like that the girls who cut his heroin are forbidden to wear anything but plastic gloves. He denies this. We met for a drink Swimsaway and I, talked about old times.

I stole his cigars.

Evenings I was spending on the backporch in an uncomfortable deck chair until it was too dark to see. I liked watching Short Pants and Fury side by side on a branch of the yew tree piercing one another's hearts with fiery love and doing that grooming thing on one another's heads, lifting each feather and twisting it sideways then laying it down. Good for the feathers. They took turns. He always finished by tweaking a point very precisely in the centre of each of her eyebrows. Afterwards they leaned their shoulders together and tilted their heads at a common angle as if pondering the same piece of air. Is it George Eliot who says that if we could pay enough attention to the world to hear the grass grow and the squirrel's heart beat, we would die of the roar of it - no, I looked it up, she says "die of that roar which lies on the other side of silence." Melodramatic but she's onto something. The silence is where to start. It's not the caaawing and the haaawing and the flap and din of other creatures that is completely mysterious, it's when they sit silent staring at the same piece of air.

Swimsaway's cigars are *Romeo y Julieta Mini* (SMOKING KILLS) *Cigarritos* from Havana. Back in the beginning, when Swimsaway and Tiplady were still colleagues, that is, one game in town and Swimsaway working for Tiplady as a kind of mid-level manager, they had a big falling-out over the cigars. Tiplady went vegan and prohibited smoke everywhere in his operation, the cars, the kitchen, the factory, the library, the clothing of employees. A soupçon of tolerance would have gone a long way for Tiplady at that time but you know what new vegans are like. Anyway Swimsaway felt he was at the top of his jump and he jumped. All this to say that *Romeo y Julieta Minis* with their trademark maroon-striped packaging and inset embossed goldleaf portrait of Romeo promising the moon to Juliet on the balcony would have been immediately recognizable to Tiplady when he pried open his week's supply of homeopathic remedies and saw that telltale glint of maroon and gold. We had arranged the pills and tinctures in an attractive radial pattern around the cigars and stuck the label with 800-number (ADDICTED? WE CAN HELP!) to the inside of the box lid.

Tiplady came out onto the porch.

He had a look on his face of a shout-out gone wrong, of deep person-to-person disappointment. People always said this about him, the personal touch, made you want to be on his team, build up the brand, crack his smile. He had on blue silk pajamas. The big creamy hands hung down like paws. And because he is so big I didn't notice the bodyguard emerge and stand behind him. I was crouched in the hawthorn hedge at the turn of the drive, my coactivists roosting somewhere above and if I'd seen the guard, if I'd tuned in the night-mare, if I'd had my coffee yet, I would have jumped up and warned her not to. But Fury took one look at that big blue silk gameboard and came plunging towards him with a loud crow sound (*haaaaaaaaaw*) that hung only a second, transected in air by the hot little zip of a bullet and she dropped.

Nobody moved.

Then everybody moved.

The bodyguard shoved Tiplady inside, hustled in after him and slammed the door. I thought Fury had fallen on the far side of the driveway somewhere. When I arrived Short Pants was circling. He made a low sound I never heard before, the tiniest font on the font list, then descended to the body which was lying on a speed bump in the driveway with its head pointing uphill. He pecked around the body two or three times and pulled once on the wing, still making that weird microscript sound. He pulled again on the wing and kept pulling until he had reoriented the body with its head downhill. He waited, watched. The body did not move. He turned and flew off. I approached closer. There was not much blood. A single neat hole through the cerebellum at the back of the skull.

Maybe the crow thing to do would have been to leave it as carrion. But I buried the body below the yew tree in my backyard. After a few days I gave up hoping for Short Pants to reappear at the bleakporch for bleaktoast from the bleakrailing. I continued to see him in trees around town, with a dishevelled appearance even when sitting still. He seemed more thoughtful, this may be a projection on my part. We want to believe that other creatures grieve like we do. Have we any proof or knowledge of this? Not really. Do we understand how we ourselves grieve? Not really. Grief is big, grief is little, grief is cranky and comes at the wrong time, usually disguised as something else. Chemically, a conspiracy of hormones, opioids and dopamine in the forebrain. I have a sense most grief is also deeply and horribly humorous but we're not supposed to say so. Aspirin for travellers, grief.

On my way to bike class this past Saturday, the guy is on the wall as usual. He has acquired a friend. Short Pants beside him on the wall. They both sit silent, looking off. I feel questions flooding my mind and stop on the path. I've been a scientist all my life, a moderately successful Aristotelian-type person, understanding human existence as a set of questions to which there are answers. I am determined to know who the guy is, and if he's the same guy that used to sit on the wall before *bloodmeal*, and if he is the same guy how he survived all that, and if he isn't what does he know about it, and how has he come to co-opt my best crow friend, and how does this crow make his decisions, and what had the crow thought of me, or was he even aware of me at all - were the crow and the guy aware of me at all as something more than a shape on the landscape. I am hopping and popping with scientific method, I am ready for final realities. Then Short Pants moves his eye onto me. And the signal turns inside out. His awareness of me, my awareness of him, their awareness of each other, a bead of electricity speeds down some axon in my brain and these three separate accountabilities seem all at once indistinguishable, one very old, very early lament in which we all have a part, one same uncomprehending core. I have always felt stunted by my own loneliness but now this strikes me as inaccurate, or the answer to a question that has not been asked. What do answers answer anyway. They fit onto questions like a stocking onto a leg but the bloodstains still refuse to evaporate. The crow and the guy on the wall and me, travellers all, what closes its lips on us, the big secret if there is a secret, I relinquish all right to. The pair of them are leaning their heads at a similar angle, watching the same piece of air, as I follow the path to the street and go my way.

THRET

Part III: SWIMMING IN HÖLDERLIN

When I remember that time now it is in layers, I move through the layers, I move through the layers and I find one connected to another by staircases that surprise me because I didn't build any staircases. Staircases became the most important part of my reasoning about all of it. I would never use an audio tape recorder or a video tape recorder, a taped conversation functions entirely on one plane. This seems to me to lack accuracy. What I mean by accuracy is hard to sum up. There is a sentence of Hölderlin's that fell out of a book of fragments of his that I read once and then I couldn't find the book again. A sentence using the verb "to swim" in the passive voice, as in:

Mein Herz ist schwimmt in Zeit.

My heart is swimmed in time.

This sentence seems to me an example of accuracy.

any
what kind of pillow do you prefer
you should feel sorry for them
what kind of pillow do you prefer
sexy
what kind of pillow do you prefer
my real hidden life
what kind of pillow do you prefer
I move past these things
what kind of pillow do you prefer
I move past these feelings
what kind of pillow do you prefer
I am not familiar with this tool
what kind of pillow do you prefer
once I slept in a contrabass case maybe I
what kind of pillow do you prefer
no pillow

"WE'VE ONLY JUST BEGUN"

They got into our car at a stoplight. It was cold. We never lock the doors in back. There were two of them. At the apartment they terrorized us. It took all day, most of the night. There was beating and thrashing and scorn and damage and fear. Sounds I didn't know came out of us. Above all it was boring. In the sense it was all actions and all bad, there is no life of the mind available amid beating and thrashing and scorn and damage and fear, no space at the back of oneself to go to and think anything else. Long stretches of boredom fill up with something like thinking but there is nothing to think except what it is, what it is to be in this, and what it is to be in this is simply and utterly nothing but what it is, no volume around it, no beach, no reverie. At one point Washington raised his arms to me and blood ran down both arms to the floor. I watched it hit the tiles, it would have been something to think about, cleaning blood off tiles. Sometimes it's better to just replace them. Eventually in fact that's what we would do, replace the white ones. We kept the black ones, which were sort of speckled anyway. But "eventually" is not a concept of mind that exists amid beating and thrashing and scorn and damage and fear. Even when they had Washington dance in the red-hot shoes I wasn't imagining analogies, Snow White, I was soaked into Washington's dread, it had no edge. That is what boredom is, the moment with no edge.

To survive you need an edge.

One of them seemed to have the name Grimaldi. *I'm slipping*, Grimaldi said every so often in a breaking-apart voice and the other guy would cross the room and stand close to him and murmur. Then they returned to what they'd been doing, breaking glass, making sandwiches, whatever it was. Washington had blacked out by this time, he didn't hear it or see it, I was on the floor with little holes burned in me but otherwise okay, pretending my hands were still tied although they weren't, watching for the edge.

I'm slipping is what I thought he was saying but I couldn't quite hear, it might have been *I'm leaking* or *I'm lingering*. There it was, the edge. He sounds like one of the undead, I said to myself. Now I don't believe in the undead, I'm a scientist, but numbers of people do and it stands to reason that among them are those who claim they *are* the undead and on that account fear leaking, lingering, perhaps slipping. They are people snapped shut on themselves. *Don't fall asleep yet.* Their voices seemed made of wood or blows falling on rotten wood. If I moved, he laid his lash onto me, the one called Grimaldi, it was a length of plastic skipping rope he wore draped around his neck, sandwich in the other hand. His colleague was looking through our tea cupboard, Grimaldi came over, they were grunting and flailing and Grimaldi with the end of his lash knocked a tin off the counter, Formosa Oolong, it crashed to the floor, bounced. He cursed. Washington's eyes flapped open like a soul on a clothesline.

How blue are Washington's eyes and what a good thing it is. Like sudden oceans. Like the shadow at the back of each wave, after the fresh collapse. Blue as blue lane lines on the bottom of a blue swimming pool. Blue as the Atlantic from 30,000 feet. Gatorade blue, salt-lick blue, satellite blue. Satellites aren't blue. I overdo analogies, I lay it on. Washington's the opposite, subtle, skittish. We met on a bus in northern Greece, a vacation tour. Everyone else on the bus was Chinese. I don't recall why I took the Chinese tour and I never asked Washington why he did.

Our guide was perplexed but valiant and translated all her monologues into shrill unusual English. Her name was Ling. I wondered idly where Ling got her English until the day - it was a long apathetic day of mountain switchbacks and hollow clouds leading to early dinner at an olive-oil factory managed by Ling's cousin - when she unfurled the microphone and turned up the volume, already quite high, to favour us with the entire repertoire of Karen Carpenter. She smiled hard while singing. All this sentimental material I could mention to our couples therapist next time we met was flowing across the front of my mind while at the back I rummaged for anything I knew about the undead. Bad walkers? Brain-eaters? What else? But now he was frowning at me. You have a problem, I said. Need to piss, said Grimaldi. I gestured with my forehead in a down-the-hall direction. Off he went, sidling and ducking. He forgot his lash.

I saw Washington notice this, the lash. I lay back on the floor in a posture of reflection. I was in physical pain. From the pain came anxiety crawling out all over the place. A hot-and-cold-at-once anxiety on little childhood currents, starting up everywhere in body and mind, tingling every follicle. It is the vagus nerve organizes such reactions. I was mentally following the path of the vagus nerve around my body and seeking to quiet it when a cry broke through my thought from the direction of the bathroom. Grimaldi had met Rocket.

We keep Rocket in the bathroom. He likes to nest in a pile of towels and have easy access to the bathtub, filled. A python bathes most of the day when he isn't sleeping or otherwise busy. Rocket has a calm and accepting nature generally but snakes don't see very well and have no ear canals at all. They navigate chiefly by smell. So when a scent triggers the feeding response the next thing that moves is food. Perhaps Grimaldi ought not to have wandered into Rocket's environs with a sandwich in one hand. They were in close communion when they toppled out of the bathroom. Grimaldi's cries tore the air and a terrible smell came off him. Pythons subdue their prey by wrapping the upper torso of the victim and tightening the coils gradually. Constriction has as its main purpose the reshaping of the victim into a narrow oblong package able to be swallowed, preferably alive. Items up to the size of a small antelope can be dealt with in this way. Grimaldi was, as it happens, too big to be swallowed by Rocket but he did not know this and Rocket was proceeding with zeal, hence Grimaldi's repeated cries of *Hack the thing! Hack it off me!*

Meanwhile I was starting to focus on the relationship between these two guys. The other still wearing his big KGB sunglasses. I remembered thinking *he looks like Putin* when he got into the car all those hours ago. Rescuing Grimaldi was evidently a low priority for Putin at this point. From where he sat on the La-Z-Boy he aimed a command across the room. *Machine down, Grimaldi, machine down.* His voice was like feces, if feces had a sound, if feces *were* a sound and I know what this would be from dreams I've had since then in which his bottom-of-the-shit-barrel voice is a dark soundtrack. At the same time, I'd noticed earlier, Putin had no smell. A sort of iridescence came out of him and stayed on the air.

The big KGB sunglasses turned in my direction. *Get it off him.* Well, ordinarily this would have been difficult because the way to deconstruct a python is to have person A hold its head while person B uncoils the coils one by one and loops them onto the floor, however, at the sound of the other guy's voice Grimaldi's entire body had gone limp and seemed to shrink, so suddenly that Rocket lost his grip. The snake paused, then slid off across the floor and up the fire screen to the mantelpiece. Grimaldi lay silent and jerking a bit. By now I was sure his relation to the other guy was that of personal slave, with Putin controlling his mind by keeping him drugged to the eyeballs in the zombie tradition. Grimaldi had lost one shoe and one sock in the fracas with Rocket. It was a long white foot like a rabbit's. Covered all over the sole with weird abrasions as if he had walked on ground glass or some very spiny thistles. I recognized standard zombie-enslaving procedure (or at least the theory of it that was current when I studied pharmacology some years ago): an abrasive residue like glass is mixed with *datura stramonium* (extract of the puffer fish) and put in the shoe of the victim. Poison burns into the bloodstream through the abraded skin of the foot and stuns the poor bastard's metabolism, sending his inner manikin screaming down to the back corner of his soul where it crouches and waits for orders. From the sole to the soul, as it were.

I gazed at the ceiling and considered S-O-U-L-S. The "soul of Greece" was a topic that often arose in conversations with elderly gentlemen in *tavernas* when Washington and I were on the China tour. These gentlemen seemed to mean something glorious and transhistorical rather than the irregular lump of solid "it" that most of us have in mind. Washington's soul I did not glimpse at all until the very end of our time in Greece. We had left the bus and travelled to Athens for our two final days. It was 42 degrees Celsius in Athens. We kept having small violent fights about small stupid things. If I describe them I will soon sound like a pressed piano key so I will merely mention that whenever Washington entered our hotel room he locked it behind him. Then closed and locked the windows. Then checked the closets. It wasn't the illogic of these actions (why check the closets *after* you've locked the door?) so much as the magnitude that bothered me. Big philosophical forms of dread, yes; poky little cretonne terrors, just depressing. And if I questioned him he'd say, *I was brought up in New York City I have these fears* and give a sort of fake gangster laugh. So there we were, our last evening in Greece, not speaking, trailing around behind an English tour group in the New Akropolis Museum of Athens.

It was wonderfully cool in the marble corridors of the Archaic and Pre-Classical Wing. Everything seemed to float, in fragments, in its own vague light. Here are broken-off pieces of buttock or torso or shoulder, draperies streaming midair and many a vacant pedestal with *Removed to the British Museum* quietly underneath. I was studying a shard of pottery on which some 7th-century BC hand had scratched a single name, over and over, the same name, and I was wondering whether a person would do that as a blessing or a curse - or maybe in hapless sorrow, like the postcard my mother got once from my brother when he was on the downslope to drugs and death. On the back of the card he'd written simply *Michael Michael Michael*, his own name, three times. Just then I heard the closing bell ring and looked round, realizing I had quite lost track of Washington. I made my way to the main exit, couldn't find him. Threaded back through the crowd to the Parthenon frieze, couldn't find him. Dashed around the gift shop, nothing. Returned to the main exit and lingered there until firmly ejected by a guard.

Outside it was darkening. I walked toward Kolonaki Square. Sat down on a stone bench. Small lighted kiosks were offering gelato and ices all along the boulevard. The heat hung in shreds. I watched people drift past, talking busily, everyone in pairs or groups. Feeling ugly and sweaty and lonely and snubbed I closed my eyes. Flashes of accident, explosion, tragedy, flying home with his coffin crossed my mind. Where had he put our passports? How much money was left? Should I call the police? What's the Greek for *police*? Fear crashed in waves in me, dropped me off cliffs. Minutes, centuries passed. I took off my glasses, smudgy with heat and despair, was searching my pockets for something to clean them when a person sat down on my bench, took my glasses from me and polished one lens then the other with a handkerchief from his breast pocket. A familiar Washington-fresh-linen smell rose around me. There comes a moment you realize other people are not interchangeable. *I looked for you!* I said and suddenly wept. He wept too. Later that night he gave me the poem he'd composed in the café at the New Akropolis Museum. He said it was a *found poem* and I said, *Good I'm a found person*. Using a red pencil he had circled all the past participles in the New Akropolis official museum guide.

Adapted
Balanced
Blown up
Bombarded
    Climbed
    Contested
    Converted
    Demolished
        Drilled
        Encroached on
        Excavated
        Fortified
            Hunted
            Kept secret
            Not planned
            Occupied
                Painted
                Partly planned
                Planned but never built
                Polluted
                    Prohibited
                    Refurbished
                    Revered
                    Rock-cut
                        Sketched
                        Sold
                        Sprung
                        fully-
              armed
              Tested
              superbly
              To be continued

It's framed now over our kitchen stove, with a title taken from Ling's repertoire. It was I who alphabetized. But I digress.

Kiss me, Grimaldi. The voice ran hot across the room and into Grimaldi's pooled limbs, organizing them instantly the way a coat hanger organizes a coat. Grimaldi scuttled over the floor and began pressing kisses to the toe of Putin's boot, a dark leather boot stitched with tiny mirrors, a voice seeming to come from the boot. *What is the kiss for, Grimaldi?* Grimaldi: *To buy love.* Putin: *What are the mirrors for?* Grimaldi: *To bend evil.* Putin: *What are the scissors for?* Grimaldi: *To cut me if I sin.*

Now I myself saw no scissors in evidence but neither was the kitchen floor covered in water and so Putin's next command - *Walk in the water, Grimaldi* - indicated a private slave code. Grimaldi got to his feet. He looked around wildly. He was very young, I hadn't noticed this before. His eyes were holes in his head. But Grimaldi was not seeing in the outward direction, something had reversed the function, his eyes only registered what or who was looking *at him*. Shame eyes. *Time to cha-cha*, said Putin. Suddenly I was afraid. There was endgame in the air. *How many kinds of kisses are there, Grimaldi?* said Putin. *Nine kinds*, Grimaldi answered, for some reason whispering. Putin: *Use number six.* Grimaldi began to move.

Pity is a corrosive substance. I've learned to avoid it in my work (I work in a lab). I can't love everyone, I can't give back their prayers. As Grimaldi began to move he forgot his one foot was bare and his traction unequal. The left foot slid fast on the floor and he stumbled forward. He stumbled heavily. He looked foolish. He looked like he knew he looked foolish. He looked like my brother. Pity came over me in a rush. There's not much to know about my brother except when he was alive we had a charged speechless relationship like a vacuum tube. To me (I was younger) his life always seemed to be falling apart - rented rooms, crap jobs, skinny girls, deals that fell through, guys who betrayed him, everything betrayed him. But it wasn't his fault. It was never his fault. He'd come home after fights, betrayed and bloody and we patched him up. My mother patched him up. I watched from the stairs. His broken face, his whole surface throbbing with shame - I hated watching but I couldn't stop.

When Grimaldi stumbled and his shame eyes swallowed the room in all directions, my hands reached out to him. What was I thinking? My brother and I never embraced, kissed, hugged, we weren't that kind of family, except the day - I recall a rainy Saturday - he stood before me in the kitchen in tears because his girlfriend was knocked up and needed cash. I was important that day. I pitied him and gave him cash. Those were the deepest feelings we got to. Years later when he died drunk in a bathroom in Europe I realized I had had no real interest in or compassion for him, just this weird sibling dissolve at the edge where my personality met his, this smudging of two selves into one. But a dark form shimmered past my visual field on the left.

Rocket was on the move.

I could see the snake's tongue flicking in and out. Snakes, as I've said, learn the world by smelling - that is, through the tongue, which is covered with sensory corpuscles able to carry the slightest trace of information back to the palate and thence to the brain. But Rocket had descended the mantelpiece and paused, he needed more data. By laying his lower jaw on the floor and picking up ground-borne vibrations he could chart his course precisely. He was charting for Putin, who had been standing by the door to the balcony, was now stepping out onto the balcony, humming to himself and doing a bit of cha-cha, a little this way, a little that, lightly absorbed in his own trance, his body moving like a scarf dropped through air onto water and turning with the current, coolly turning. He was a beautiful dancer. Rocket was up his leg, across the torso and wrapping his neck before you could say *stand-up comedian*. Putin cha-chaed no more that day.

Grimaldi had subsided to the floor, confused. I think his body confused him. Air confused him. From his body and from the air was suddenly absent the entire hot horrible pressure of the other guy. Did he connect Putin's fallen form on the balcony with this absence? He turned over and lay on his back, making small sounds that were (to me) like a broom sweeping the stairs, this calm sound. When my brother died I swept the porch and the stairs all afternoon. Something about sweeping and death, it goes together. And there went Rocket gliding past in the other direction. He had an expressive look. People assume reptiles lack moral sense but that is because we make no close observation of their decisions. Rocket has a keen appreciation of the ruthlessness of men but on those rare occasions when ruthlessness abates he is moved to wonder and sympathy. He was sliding along Grimaldi's leg and up over his T-shirt into the V-shaped hollow formed by his bent arm. Here he coiled himself carefully and paused, laying his head on the edge of Grimaldi's chest with a small sigh. Grimaldi raised his head to look dazedly at the python. *Snake likes me*, he shyly shone. Then as a moonlit road he dimmed again and ghosts blew across him.

I've always felt unsatisfied with random homonyms. Words that sound alike but mean differently: let's go back to *sole* and *soul*. Linguists tell us that, given the great number of meanings we want to express in our language and the limited number of sounds we can produce with our mouths, there's nothing to puzzle about here at all.

Homonyms are inevitable. Still, perhaps you share with me a compulsion to find some primordial link between, on the one hand, being able to walk along the world on little platforms of tough flesh and, on the other hand, having a conscious, sensible or spiritual otherness aloft within your body. A primordial link between the sole and the soul is of course etymologically bogus. The two words have separate historical formations (sole of the foot deriving from Latin *solea*, "shoe or sandal," while the origins of soul as spiritual essence are quite unknown). Any overlap in sound is, scientifically speaking, a total accident.

And yet, and yet. Don't they overlap in other ways? What comes to mind are considerations of tenderness or vulnerability - where is pain felt as sharply as in the bottom of the foot if not in the spirit? Then too there's a spatial aspect. The *OED* defines "sole" as "the lower part or under surface of anything" - from a plough to a rudder to a drainpipe to a furrow to a glacier - and don't most people think of their S-O-U-L as a deep-down layer, a metaphysical substrate? In any case, the reason I mention all this is that, as I pondered the python curled in the crook of Grimaldi's arm with his smooth snaky belly exposed, I found myself staring at the perfect little soles of Rocket's feet. You almost certainly know that snakes once had feet, attached to legs, which they shed - for shame according to the book of Genesis, for mobility according to theories of natural selection. Legless a snake can travel as fast as a human, climb trees, navigate almost any horizontal trajectory and swim more gracefully than a fish. The python does retain vestigial traces of hind leg, those two tiny protuberances on the underbelly that poke up like the soles of forgotten feet. Every time I noticed them I felt strange, a wind rushed by. Is there such a thing as evolutionary pathos? Two bumps of bone evoking a

130-million-year-ago hesitation in whatever random pro-
cess or brooding intelligence was nudging creation along
at the time. Snakes also carry inside them the remains of
a pelvis. Does this make it uncomfortable to grind along
the floor on your belly? But snakes don't feel pain the
way we do, do they? Snakes have this in common with
zombies, or so I have heard, although, my real opinion
is, even from our lofty place on the ladder of Being, we
don't really know what snakes feel or zombies think. We
don't know who has a soul and who doesn't. There's no
test for soul. You may be familiar with the story of Dr.
Duncan MacDougall, who in 1901 attempted to discover
the weight of the S-O-U-L by calculating the mass lost by
a human body at the moment of death. His experiments
gave him an average result of 21 grams but these could
never be replicated by anyone else and are regarded as
scientifically meaningless. More recently an Oregon
rancher tried a similar experiment on 8 sheep, 3 lambs
and a goat, who all *gained* weight at death. He continues
to puzzle over this result.

Scientists in general regard the soul-test as a futile
research. I'm not so sure. I think there are clues. I don't
mean some bluebird that soars through the room and
keeps going and ends up in heaven. On the other hand,
why was that window open?

So finally this long day and night come to an end. Hours
later. We are sitting at the kitchen table. Washington has
the lash in his hands, vaguely unfolding and refolding it
around its plastic handles. A cold dirty yellow dawn has
strayed in. On the other side of the table is a sort of pile of
Grimaldi, adrift in his hoodie, face absent. When the police
arrive they will remove Putin's body and take Grimaldi
into custody. He seems quiescent. I think about trying to

question him. He looks at me. His eyes burn the air, the air falls apart. Then he lays back his head and the hoodie slips down and he shrieks - it's his broom-sweeping-the-stairs sound, possibly a laugh.

I hate this laugh.

I hate sitting here. Grimaldi sinks back into his hoodie. Well then, I say. Does something need to happen now? Prayer? Sobbing? Laceration? Some kind of exchange between me and this blind beaten person? It is black in me how much I want this. Yet my theories stop short of him. The story is exhausting. And a part of me thinks, Why not just let Rocket have another go at murdering him? But Rocket's made his own decision. When the police officer bustles in and out of the bathroom to take a piss right beside his head. Rocket does not even look up.

what is your philosophy of time
am not familiar with this tool
do you neaten your bed in the morning
he dog would like it
do you neaten your
colonization drops down its bars
what is your philosophy of time
he dog would like it
what is your philosophy of time
darker in the nights

WHAT I LIKE ABOUT YOU, BABY

ex-lover 1
ex-lover 2

1	you smell damp, is it raining?
2	nice and dry in here
1	two hundred seats not even half-full
2	Japanese film week?
1	funny how Americans dislike subtitles
2	you said this one's a *film noir*?
1	*what I like about you, baby, is you're rock bottom*
2	and what I like about *film noir* is -
1	no one ever reads a book, no one ever cleans their teeth, no one is ever happy except pouring a drink
2	and they pour lots of drinks
1	*is there a way to win? no, baby, but there's a way to lose more slowly*
2	oh stop
1	remember that one we saw where the guy lost his gun?
2	lost what?
1	we saw it here, I'm pretty sure
2	here? impossible
1	the first time we came here, yes
2	all those years ago? oh no
1	it was Japanese film week then too, I remember
2	I think not, no
1	it had those old-fashioned subtitles, yes
2	wait a minute, was there a phone booth?
1	subtitles went by too fast
2	I remember a scene in a phone booth, everyone sweating, crammed in a phone booth
1	that was a different movie
2	but remember phone booth?
1	no it wasn't that he lost it, someone stole it from his jacket on the bus
2	stole what?

1   his gun
2   you always liked really different movies than me
1   hard not to like classic *film noir*
2   I just remember the heat, that summer wasn't it the hottest on record or
    something?
1   you mean in the movie?
2   the reason we went to that movie was the heat, to get out of the heat
1   no, it was fall, I'm sure it was fall, I've always associated us coming here
    with leaves falling
2   really?
1   yes, leaves falling and that haiku poem about having no home
2   what poem?
1   was it a haiku? Rilke? no, I don't know, I lost the book
2   anyway, the phone booth scene was the best part
1   that was a different movie
2   I don't think so
1   I've been remembering that fall, we used to meet in movie theaters
2   we met in the underpass
1   your parents didn't like me
2   we met in the park
1   what was that movie, I adored that movie, not the *film noir*, the other one
2   the love suicide?
1   lovers running in a field
2   and the raspberries stain her dress
1   just the slide of those facts
2   was it a joke, were we mad?
1   sometimes love is a mess
2   but a solid mess
1   I brought my service revolver
2   who paid for the hotel?
1   that night, was it a joke?
2   you pointed it at my heart
1   I remember the smell of leaves
2   I'd do anything you said
1   we met anywhere it was dark

2   there were headlights going by
1   you had your mother's credit card
2   you said love should be damnation
1   you said *I'm doing this for you*
2   there were headlights in your eyes
1   the chill smell of leaves
2   just the slide of these facts
1   was I wrong, were you laughing?
2   you had it wrapped in a fancy napkin from the hotel
1   it was all so weird and simple
2   you were maybe a bit off-balance then, a bit delirious
1   a bit deformed
2   or was that love?
1   can love deform?
2   some sort of shadow invading your soul or -
1   the fact is
2   we had a pact
1   there's just her running in a field with the light behind her
2   we could never agree
1   not much dialogue at all
2   on who would go first
1   and the light is coming out of everything
2   and he lifts his gun and shoots her through the heart
1   the fact is
2   a movie's just bright things and dark things changing places
1   subtitles went by too fast
2   so what about the phone booth scene?
1   that was a different movie
2   I'm going for popcorn
1   quiet, it's starting

what is your philosophy of mine
the kind of pillow one does not worry about
what kind of pillow do you prefer
the sea

WHAT TO SAY OF THE ENTIRETY

What to say of the entirety. The entirety should be smaller. Small enough to say something about. Humans? What if the guy you're hanging up by his thumbs already has a razorplague of painapples roaming his chest inside. Do you regard that as his own fault? Do you really need to make it worse? Do you think of yourself as a well? Of course these are separate questions. Like dead salmon and copper-mine tailings, separate. So these separations, this anaesthesia, we should ponder a bit. Humans. What can you control? Wrong question. Can you treat everything as an emergency without losing the reality of time, which continues to drip, laughtear by laughtear? Where to start? Start in the middle (and why) so as not to end up there, where for example the torture report ended up after all those years of work. You have to know what you want, know what you think, know where to go. New York City actually. Here we are. Trucks crash by. Trucks are louder in the rain, or was that another row of doors slammed by gods? They're soaked, the gods, they've tucked their toes up on their thrones as if they don't know why this is happening. Poor old coxcombs.

what is your philosophy of time
power
what is your philosophy of time
for a year I made homemade toothpaste

Todtnauberg

THE STORY SO FAR

Heidegger was a committed Nazi from 1933 until who knows when. He avoided speaking publicly about this. In 1966 Celan gave a reading at Freiburg University. Heidegger sat in the front row. Next day Celan visited Heidegger at his mountain hut on Todtnauberg and wrote an inscription in the guestbook. What else passed between them is unknown. After returning from the mountain Celan wrote a poem called "Todtnauberg" about the day. In 1970 he killed himself.

Snow

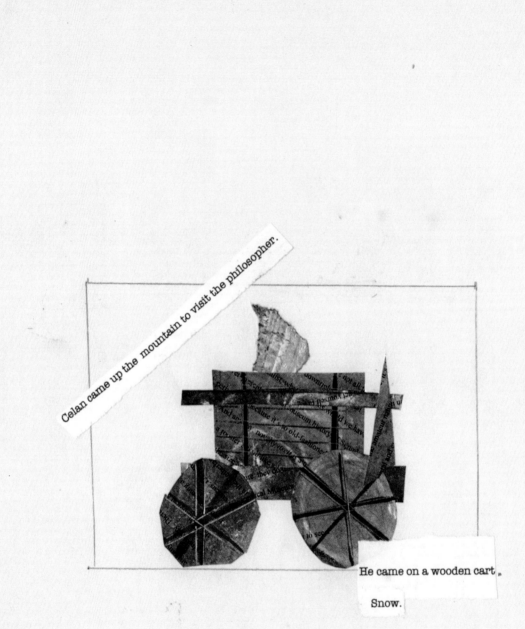

Celan came up the mountain to visit the philosopher.

He came on a wooden cart.

Snow.

He felt ashamed.

Shame is unreasonable.

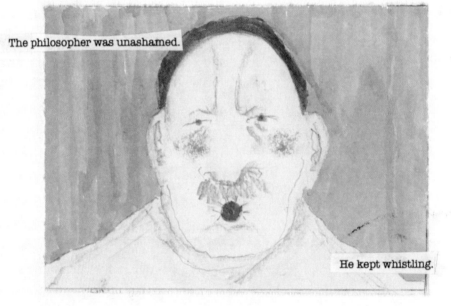

The philosopher was unashamed.

He kept whistling.

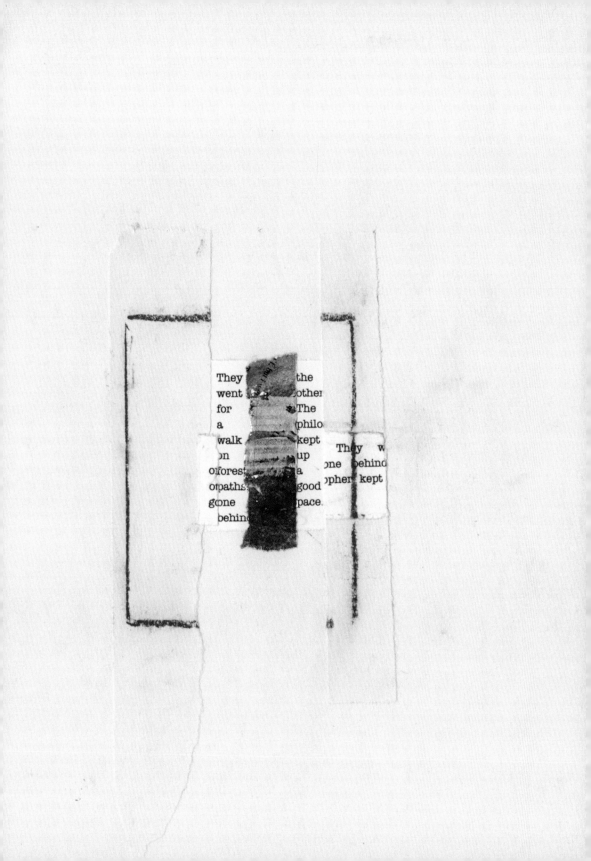

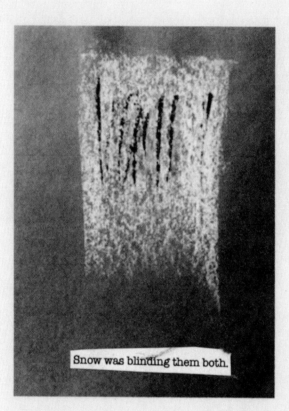

Snow was blinding them both.

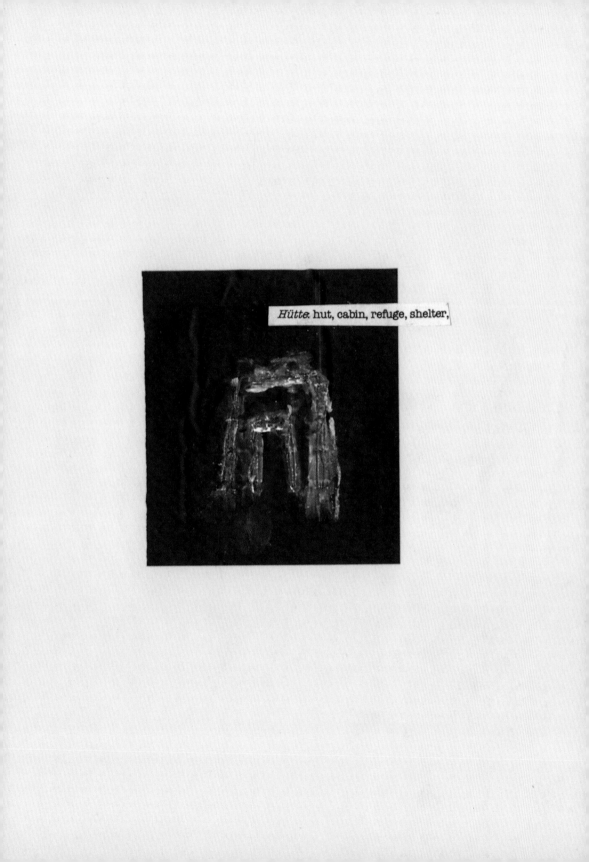

Hütte: hut, cabin, refuge, shelter,

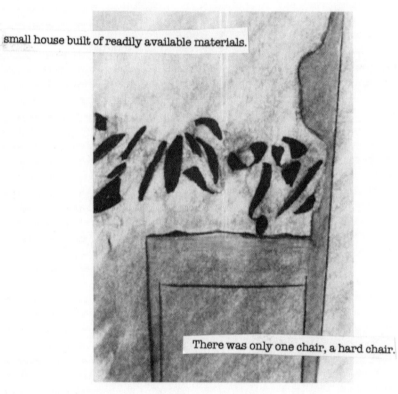

small house built of readily available materials.

There was only one chair, a hard chair.

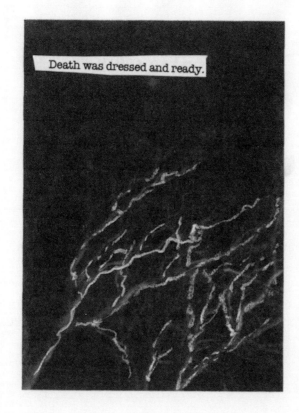

Celan loaded his cart and started back down.

WRONG NORMA

Wrong night, wrong city, wrong movie, wrong ambulances caterwauling past and drowning out wrong dialogue of wrong Norma Desmond, what could be more wrong she's the same age as me this tilted wreck with deliquescent chin, I turn it off, eat soup and read a novel. Thoughts trickle in and out. No one phones. I am safe but that won't last. I drift to the past, even 20 years ago wasn't it possible to be pure? To just close the door and think about one thing, the moon, curbs, Etruria. The self wins anyway. The "s" in self wins. I used to love making "s" in cursive style on the blackboard at school, it's different every time, every shell on the beach, do they even have blackboards, teach cursive, anymore? I can't wait for morning. Sunday morning on West 3rd my favourite time. No cars. Branches stark. Daybreak greenish and cold and on a rooftop across from me the legendary water towers of New York City, the giant white smoke Miltoning to heaven.

1 : ABCDEF

2 : FAEBDC

3 : CFDABE

4 : ECBFAD

5 : DEACFB

6 : BDFECA

7 : use all 6nd words Sonscha